FAMILIES

AT THE

CROSSROADS

B E Y O N D

T R A D I T I O N A L

& M O D E R N

O P T I O N S

RODNEY CLAPP

InterVarsity Press
DOWNERS GROVE, ILLINOIS, USA
LEICESTER, ENGLAND

InterVarsity Press
P.O. Box 1400, Downers Grove, IL 60515, USA
38 De Montfort Street, Leicester LE1 7GP, England

©1993 by Rodney Clapp

InterVarsity Press®, U.S.A., is the book-publishing division of InterVarsity Christian Fellowship®, a student movement active on campus at hundreds of universities, colleges and schools of nursing in the United States of America, and a member movement of the International Fellowship of Evangelical Students. For information about local and regional activities, write Public Relations Dept., InterVarsity Christian Fellowship, 6400 Schroeder Rd., P.O. Box 7895, Madison, WI 53707-7895.

Inter-Varsity Press, England, is the book-publishing division of the Universities and Colleges Christian Fellowship (formerly the Inter-Varsity Fellowship), a student movement linking Christian Unions in universities and colleges throughout the United Kingdom and the Republic of Ireland, and a member movement of the International Fellowship of Evangelical Students. For information about local and national activities, write to UCCF, 38 De Montfort Street, Leicester LE1 7GP.

Scripture quotations, unless otherwise noted, are from the New Revised Standard Version of the Bible, copyright 1989 by the Division of Christian Education of the National Council of the Churches of Christ in the U.S.A., and are used by permission.

Acknowledgment is hereby made for the use of the following copyrighted material:

Figure 1, on page 18, taken from David Harvey, The Condition of Postmodernity *(Oxford: Basil Blackwell, 1989). Used by permission.*

Excerpt from One Fish, Two Fish, Red Fish, Blue Fish *by Dr. Seuss. Copyright 1960 by Theodor S. Geisel and Audrey S. Geisel. Copyright renewed 1988 by Audrey S. Geisel and Carl Zobell, trustees under the trust agreement dated August 27, 1984. Reprinted by permission of Random House, Inc.*

Excerpt from "The Country of Marriage" in The Country of Marriage, *copyright ©1971 by Wendell Berry, reprinted by permission of Harcourt Brace & Company.*

USA ISBN 0-8308-1655-0

UK ISBN 0-85110-994-2

Printed in the United States of America ♾

Library of Congress Cataloging-in-Publication Data

Clapp, Rodney
    Families at the crossroads: beyond traditional roles and modern
options/Rodney Clapp.
        p.   cm.
    Includes bibliographical references.
    ISBN 0-8308-1655-0
    1. Family—United States. 2. Family—United States—Religious
aspects.   I. Title.
HQ536.C53   1993
306.85'0973—dc20   *93-21559*
                                                             CIP

British Library Cataloguing in Publication Data

A catalogue record for this book is available from the British Library.

15	14	13	12	11	10	9	8	7	6	5	4	3	2	1
04	03	02	01	00	99	98	97	96	95	94	93			

In memory of Everett Clapp, 1937-1982:

Christian, father, cowboy, storyteller,
champion of the underdog.

Dig the spurs deep, Dad—
I'm riding right behind you.

CHAPTER ONE

POSTMODERNITY:
A NEW BATTLEFIELD
FOR THE WAR
OVER THE FAMILY

•

*What we are looking for . . . is not a way to keep dry
above the waves of relativity, but a way to stay within our
bark, barely afloat and sometimes awash amidst those
waves, yet neither dissolving into them nor being carried
only where they want to push us.*

John Howard Yoder, *The Priestly Kingdom*

Once, studying inside a Chicago seminary library on a bitter winter day, I looked out the window and saw two African women inching along an icy sidewalk. Apparently new to the climate, they were clad brightly but vulnerably in thin cotton robes. Their robes whipped in the wind and lashed their ankles as they clung to one another and moved, painstakingly, toward shelter. As they came closer, their faces betrayed shock and fear. Then I realized they had probably never before walked on ice. For years they had lived in a more hospitable climate and always trusted the ground beneath their feet. But on this day, amazingly, the earth had coated itself with a slippery, treacherous surface.

Vulnerable, surprised, betrayed—I think these women felt all these things. For them, the very foundation of the world, the ground they walked upon, had changed overnight. Evangelical Christians, in their championing of what they call the traditional family, often feel the same way. I would not go so far as to say that twentieth-century evangelicals consider the family the foundation of the world, the ground they walk upon. But they have granted family an importance that, say, their Puritan forebears would never have imagined. Sociologist James Davison Hunter suggests that within today's evangelical circles family has achieved a significance "perhaps never before seen." He quite correctly observes that "the family has in recent times become a symbol to Evangelicals, a symbol of social stability and traditional moral virtue." In a world that values flux over stability and an array of moral options over traditional virtue, the evangelical symbol of stability and virtue appears to be treading on slippery ice indeed.

It's not as if the family never had troubles before. But scant decades ago, most Westerners agreed that lifelong monogamy was ideal, that mothers should stay home with children, that premarital sex was to be discouraged, that heterosexuality was the unquestioned norm and that popular culture should not corrupt children. Today not a single one of these expectations is uncontroversial.

Accordingly, evangelical books on the family reflect a profound sense of threat and peril. Tim LaHaye writes *The Battle for the Family.* James Dobson and Gary Bauer publish *Children at Risk: The Battle for the Hearts and Minds of Our Kids.* In his book peeking ahead to *The New Millennium,* evangelist and presidential candidate Pat Robertson includes a chapter entitled "The Assault on the Family."

In books, and on radio and television, these men and other evangelical family champions worry over a fairly consistent list of concerns. They criticize public schools for suspect curriculum and teaching methods. They note alarming divorce rates. They decry movies, music and television programs that frighten children and expose them to explicit sex and violence. They abhor the spread of the gay rights movement and the rise of feminism. They place in opposition to all these things what they call the "traditional," "biblical" and even "natural" family—the nuclear family consisting of a heterosexual couple and their children, in which the husband and father is the breadwinner and the wife and mother manages home and childrearing.

American evangelicals often speak in the same breath about the survival of the traditional family, capitalism and the United States of America. Stumping for the presidency in 1988, Jack Kemp visited evangelical churches with a triad of "great issues": "Western Judeo-Christian values," "family and family values" and the free-enterprise system. These three, he said, stand or fall together. Evangelist James Robison likewise relates faith and family to the "American way of life," suggesting that the enemies of America attack the home and family in order to destroy the nation. The country is vulnerable through the family "because all America has become—a strong, thriving nation, full of creativity, variety, and uniqueness—owes itself to the foundational influence of marriage and the family."

As we will see, what evangelicals call the "traditional family" is in fact the bourgeois or middle-class family, which rose to dominance in the nineteenth century—not accidentally alongside capitalism and, a little later, America the ascendant world power. In this sense the typical evangelical account is accurate in linking family, free enterprise and "traditional" values. And it correctly suggests that changes in this traditional family portend changes—profound, disquieting changes—in our entire society. Consider this magisterial summary by sociologist Robert Nisbet:

We are learning just how vital has been the middle-class family, the kind of family that began to be evident in Western society in the seventeenth century and that has had extraordinary effect upon the motivations—economic, political, social, architectural, educational, and recreational—which have transformed the West since the Middle Ages. Almost all of what we are prone to call middle-class ways of behavior are in fact middle-class *family* ways of behavior. The difference is very large. We are witnessing today the maintenance of middle-class *levels* in income distribution and housing construction; but we are also witnessing the near collapse of the kind of household that for several centuries was inseparable from economic level.

The Amish Reminder

So the evangelical traditionalists are right on several counts. What they call the traditional family has been crucially important to our society. Many of this family's values will be lost if current trends continue, and the loss will be a detriment to our entire culture. And this family is now, truly, under assault. These are perilous and momentous times.

Yet if there is much to agree with in the traditionalist diagnosis, there is also much to contest in it. In these pages I will contest the glorification of the family to the point that the church is sometimes seen as the "last great stronghold of family idolatry." I will contest the presumption that the first social responsibility of the Christian is owed to his or her country rather than the church. I will contest the too-uncritical embrace of capitalism as if it somehow represented the economy of the very kingdom of God. And I will contest the assumption that the "traditional" family is the one and only "biblical" family.

In short, the chapters that follow are an attempt to tease out and move toward a more fully biblical interpretation of the Christian family's responsibilities and privileges in these foreboding but dazzling times. To achieve this, I must first bluntly challenge the evangelical traditionalist tendency to assume and assert that its conception of family is *drawn directly and without mediation from the Bible.*

The "traditional family" is not a family lifted out of the Bible's patriarchal period, its united kingdom period, its exilic and postexilic period, its early or late New Testament period, or any other period. Though certainly presented with reference to the Bible (and in some ways true to it), it is instead a family lifted out of nineteenth-century, industrialized Europe and North America.

In important respects, the "traditional family" in fact adopts family values that depart from those of the earlier evangelical heritage. For example, through much of history the family was an economically productive unit. The household was a place where husband, wife and children together farmed, did craftwork or otherwise earned their livelihood. The bourgeois or traditional family, by contrast, has lost the family's earlier function as an economically productive unit. Its main function is sentimental. It serves as haven and oasis, emotional stabilizer and battery-charger for its members. It demands that spouses and children love and trust one another, that they intensely enjoy being together.

But sentimentality was not a primary family value for those earlier evangelicals known as the Puritans. Their spouses were chosen rationally, not romantically. The Puritans carefully took into account considerations of property, piety and family interest.

Movie after movie has depicted young middle-class protagonists who want to marry someone their parents dislike. Finally, according to the usual script, Mom and Dad begin to cave in. At last they ask the crucial question: "But do you love him?" We can imagine all kinds of things, but we can't imagine marrying someone you don't already love. But the Puritans could. They did not expect affection to create the initiative for marriage. It was expected to develop after the wedding.

And though Puritans surely loved their children, we can hardly call their view of youngsters "sentimental." After the age of two, the child's salvation required that its will be broken. So Jonathan Edwards warned against the deceptively innocent appearance of children. However blameless they might seem, "if they are out of Christ, they are not [innocent] in God's sight, but are young vipers, and are infinitely more hateful than vipers." And if a child's true nature was worse than reptilian, its correction required strong measures. So in their childrearing the Puritans emphasized God's wrath and the horrors of hell. As Steven Mintz and Susan Kellogg write, "A child's willfulness could be suppressed through fierce physical beatings, exhibition of corpses, and tales of castration and abandonment."

Not valuing sentimentality and intimacy as highly as the middle-class, bourgeois or traditional family, the Puritans were also prone to emphasize the danger of loving children or spouse inordinately. So one Thomas Shepard saw in the serious illness of his child a sign that God was angry with him because of his "immoderate love of creatures and of my child especially." And during a period of devastating epidemics, Jonathan Edwards surmised that God's "Design" in visiting sickness and death on the faithful's offspring was to present a "Testimony against our Immoderate Love to, and Doating upon our Children." Another great divine, George Whitefield, could think about a potential spouse in a similar vein. During an evangelistic tour of North America, Whitefield determined not to marry, for fear of a relationship that would overcome his ardor for Christ. Later he said, "I want a *gracious woman* that is dead to everything but Jesus . . . [who] daily grants me fresh tokens of his love, and assures me that he will not permit me to fall by the hands of a woman."

With just a bit of historical digging, then, we quickly uncover some ironies. On key points, at least, some very important ancestors of today's evangelicals failed to erect or even to admire what contempo-

rary evangelicals describe as the "traditional," the "biblical" and even
the "natural" family. Were the Puritans, were Jonathan Edwards and
George Whitefield, untraditional, unbiblical, unnatural?

I, for one, would not call them any of those things. But neither would
I consult them for childrearing expertise. Instead, scratching up the
Puritan case should remind us that there is no biblical blueprint, no
once-and-for-all model, of the family.

The God of the Bible is not a philosophical construct, not an impersonal force to be dissected and manipulated. The God of the Bible is
the living, dynamic source and sustainer of all that is, who deigns to
enter history and relationship with the people Israel and the man Jesus.

So the Bible itself is not a list of abstract, timeless formulas. It simply
provides no detailed guidance or techniques, for all times and places,
on disciplining children or seeking a mate or determining whether a
wife should or should not work outside the home. Rather, the Bible is
centrally and first of all the *story* of Israel and Jesus. Beyond that, it
includes the poetry and prison letters of people who faithfully responded to that story in their own times and places.

To create and live in a truly Christian family, the church in every
generation and culture must read the biblical story anew. It must attend
closely to the poetry and prison letters (and other genres) to see how
the pioneers of the faith responded to the story in the light of the
particular challenges and privileges of their cultures. Then, without
assuming it can simply mimic the pioneers (declaring, for instance, that
all good Christians will wear sandals like Peter, or that women will
cover their heads in worship like the early Christians at Corinth), the
church must respond to the story of Israel and Jesus in the light of the
particular challenges and privileges of its own culture.

So in the chapters that follow I do not pretend that I am uncovering
biblical formulas for the family that should be put forth and followed

in all times and places. I do not believe in universal, abstract rules or techniques that can be presented and understood *free of a context* (which is to say, a story). The whole idea of such things is in fact the invention of particular philosophers (such as Immanuel Kant) living in particular cultures (German, French, English) in particular times (the seventeenth century and following). What I offer, instead, is a reading of the biblical story with special relevance to the Western Christian family in the late twentieth and early twenty-first centuries. My aim is to discover what purposes and hopes our families should assume to remain faithful. Remaining faithful means witnessing to the living truth of the God revealed in Scripture. Witnessing means incarnating the family in peculiar shapes and rich practices *that can only be explained by resorting to the story of Israel and Jesus Christ.*

In the process, we must resist the hasty and careless blurring of such words as *traditional, natural* and *biblical.* Such blurring has created the widespread impression that those who would question aspects of the industrial, middle-class family are disputing Scripture and departing from a way of family that is thousands of years old, even based on the order of nature itself. Too often those who dissent are dismissed as mere fashion-mongers, as modernists or secularists—fickle souls fatally susceptible to the whims of the day.

The mistake of evangelical traditionalists begins when they look around and see that the family they promote is not supported by the wider society. Then they assume that their position is "biblical," whereas positions of (apparently) more recent vintage are "cultural" and non-Christian. With the traditionalist, I reject the myth of progress and its easy assumption that the latest is necessarily the best. But note well that the traditionalist's position can be just as trendy and is certainly every bit as cultural as, say, the Christian feminist's. The difference is that the traditionalist supports trends and fashions from another decade or another century. These trends and fashions *may* have as little to do with the Christian story as any movement of the moment. The Amish stand as a vivid reminder that none of us escapes cultural influence. Their horse-drawn buggies and lantern-lighted homes are from another time but, to those of us on the outside looking in, clearly not from beyond time.

The Stumbling Giant

If our faith is not known from beyond time and our families cannot incarnate it beyond time, it is crucial that we understand the specific time we live in. As I put it earlier, the church must respond to the story of Israel and Jesus in light of the particular challenges and privileges of its culture. What are our challenges and privileges?

The contemporary world, like an uncoordinated and loosely jointed giant, hurtles headlong down a steep slope, already off balance and stumbling, maybe facing an imminent—and disastrous—fall. We live in times of incredibly rapid and prolific changes. People, products, ideas and cultures meet, mingle and mutate with dazzling speed.

To think: From the fourteenth century through much of the nineteenth, the fastest modes of transportation available were sailing ships and horse-drawn carriages. They skimmed across oceans and shot down dirt roads at a grand velocity of ten miles per hour. The mid-nineteenth century brought the invention of steam engines, and suddenly the speed of transportation increased 300 to 600 percent, with steam locomotives averaging sixty-five miles per hour and steamships thirty-six miles per hour.

Speed shrinks things. It enables people to get from one town to another, one country to another, in less time, and in that way diminishes distance, overpowers and dwarfs geography. So in the mere decades it took to perfect steamships and build railroads, the world shrank many times smaller.

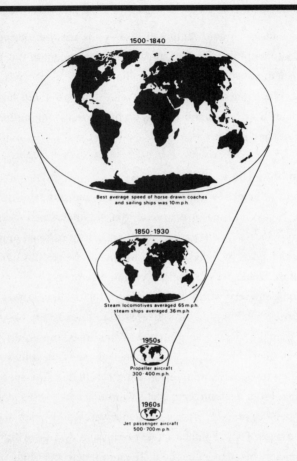

Figure 1. The Shrinking Globe 1500 to 1960

But what is steampower compared to the great bounds of speed that were gained in the mid-twentieth century? Propeller aircraft soared at three hundred to four hundred miles per hour. Before long this speed was nearly doubled, by jet passenger planes that exceed five hundred to seven hundred miles per hour. It's as if the world was the size of a softball four centuries ago, but today looms no larger than a marble.

(An exquisite blue and green marble, in fact, is exactly what the globe most resembles in photographs captured through rocketry—yet another quantum leap in speed.)

Speed shrinkage and its effects are incredible. I think even my grandparents—who tell tales of riding horseback to school, then living to leap half the continent in jet planes—can hardly begin to appreciate how much life on this earth has been altered in the course of such innovations. Trade and commerce expanded. Armies were tempted with the possibility of larger and larger empires. Missionaries discovered vast new mission fields. And of course the technology of transportation was not growing in isolation. Alongside it came the telegraph, telephone, radio and televison, each helping to shrink the world even smaller.

All of which is to say our world is much smaller and much faster than the world of, say, Christopher Columbus. In consequence, we are much more acutely aware of our differences. Hindus are no longer so obscured by thousands of miles and quaint Kiplingesque tales; now they live next door and get in line behind us at the supermarket cash register. Board a subway in London or New York, and your car alone may host representatives of three or four races, speaking in as many languages.

And in a smaller and faster world, we are much more acutely aware of change and the possibility for change. Some of the Muslims we watch on the evening news don't believe in the separation of religion and politics, and would erect entirely different economic systems from ours—rejecting, for instance, the charging of interest. The gay activist who lives down the street (or perhaps sits beside us in the pew) forcefully argues for a nontraditional sexual ethic. Some fundamentalist friends withdraw their children from public school and say that serious Christians should be home-schooling their children.

Slavery has been abolished, women and people of color have gotten the vote, polio has been virtually eliminated, a man has walked on the moon, videocassette recorders have created a whole new kind of store and market. The call of revolution—political, religious, economic, scientific, educational—surrounds us. Why, then, when change prevails everywhere and every day, should anything stay the same? Especially if someone doesn't like something the way it is?

Abruptly, zooming along in the jet plane of progress, we plunge into a dark cloud. It seems there are limits to change. People who were ready and willing to switch from a straight-edged razor to an electric shaver are not so ready to switch religions. People who admitted the obsolescence of trolley cars with only a twinge or two of nostalgia are not so apt to admit the obsolescence of their tradition's sexual ethic. None of us could stay sane in this world if we hadn't learned to embrace a great deal of change. But many of us aren't sure *everything* should change, however fast and small the world has become, however loudly the various revolutionaries are protesting. At some point we want to get out of the jet plane and plant our feet on the ground—solid ground.

So times of incredible speed and change are exciting, but they are also confusing and sometimes frightening. High in the air, hurtling to its destination, the jet plane provides a vantage point of startling clarity. We see the mountains sink and flatten into the plains, the neat brown and green squares of farmland, the city laid out with it heart-cluster of skyscrapers feeding roadways like huge bloodstreams. Speed gives us this beautiful picture, makes us feel as if nothing could be better than to just keep moving, makes us feel as if we don't need to land and belong somewhere. But of course we can't live in midair. And once we stop concentrating on speed and dip toward the ground for a closer look, the picture blurs. The mountains, the farmlands, the skyscrapers and roadways flit by indecipherably. We can pick out no landmarks, no orienting topography or buildings. At high speed, it's harder and harder to know exactly where we are and where we are going.

Then we are confused and frightened. Where will our technological power, now seemingly out of our control, take us? Nuclear weaponry could destroy the world as we know it. Holes in the ozone layer, we are told, could make a day on the beach a severe health threat. Within decades, the greenhouse effect could lead to the flooding of Manhattan. Genetic engineering could create now-inconceivable miracles—and monstrosities. This is not all. Ours is a time not only of massive and confusing technological change. A shrunken and speeding world also presents us with profound moral change. As the philosopher Charles Taylor argues, some of the most important cultural shifts of our day go deeper than technology: "What matters is that masses of people can sense moral sources of a quite different kind, ones that don't necessarily suppose a God." Certainly, we might add, sources that don't suppose the God of Israel and Jesus. And sources that do suppose a whole array of other gods.

Another Name for Nowhere
So: the Christian family is about faithfully witnessing to the love and power of God in its time and place. But if the world is changing religiously, morally, politically and scientifically at an unparalleled rate, do we know where we are? If the jet plane is flying low and the landscape rushes past us in a blur, can we name our location?

There is, in fact, a name for where we are. Several commentators have begun to call ours a *postmodern* world. The modern world, profoundly shaped by the eighteenth-century Enlightenment, was based on a deep faith in unaided human reason. Weary of religious wars, modernists assumed that reason—apart from any particular religious tradition—could provide a universal human basis for morality. From this womb liberal democracy and the modern nation-state were born. Now the world could have done with religious tribalism and all its bickering and bloodshed. Religion could be relegated harmlessly to private, individual life; the democratic state, supposedly resting on truths available to all reasonable people, would tend to public life. With this hope, and intoxicated by staggering scientific innovation, the world of modernity was one of unflagging optimism. Reason would show the way.

But the twentieth century has shattered that dream. In a single century, more people have died in wars fought in the name of nation-states than died in all the religious wars combined. As the former Union of Soviet Socialist Republics and Eastern Europe crumble into a rabble of ethnic conclaves vying for statehood, we are vividly reminded that there can be more warring nationalisms than religions.

Furthermore, the utter objectivity of science has proved illusory. What, now, can we make of "scientific" socialism, which aimed to take the USSR into a paradise on earth but instead took it to the brink of ruin? And we have learned that even the physical, empirical sciences are dependent on a certain *mythos,* an overall view of life and the cosmos that cannot itself be conclusively proven or disproven. The physical or "hard" sciences are not only born to a specific cultural milieu, but live and express themselves through that milieu. Consequently, evolution—perhaps the premier scientific truth of our time— was used to justify eugenics, racial superiority and unabashed imperialism. Darwin himself, in *The Descent of Man,* wrote that there was "apparently much truth" in the theory that America's "wonderful progress" was the result of natural selection.

My point is not that this was the only or best interpretation or application of evolution. Instead, it is simply that, from inception through implementation, evolution was and is *culturally and historically* interpreted. It, and science in general, is never extracultural, never a matter of "pure" reason that stands beyond all traditions. As Bishop

Lesslie Newbigin writes in *The Gospel in a Pluralist Society,*

> Clearly the scientific tradition as a whole, and the many concepts,
> classifications of data, and theoretical models which are the working
> tools of science form as a whole a tradition *within* which scientists
> have to *dwell* in order to do their work. Without such an enduring
> tradition, science would collapse. At any moment in history several
> parts of the tradition may be under critical review and alternatives
> may be proposed; but this critical review would be impossible with-
> out the a-critical acceptance of the tradition as a whole. The progress
> of science depends, therefore, on the authority of this tradition.

In fact, reason itself has a history, is part of a tradition; it springs from
particular cultures, specific *mythoi* or worldviews. The postmodern
discovery is that the great guiding light of reason, when seen through
the prism of different cultures, diffracts and divides into competing
lights. The underlying faith and hope of modernity has been shattered,
so that we truly live in times of "religious" crisis. That is, there is no
widespread agreement on what is our ultimate good, the common end
or goal of our society. And we now know that reason cannot stand above
and apart from the fray to provide a common good. Consequently we
fight endlessly over abortion, over homosexuality, over what genuine
justice is, over the meaning of family itself.

True to our general climate of factionalism and debate, there is no
one accepted definition of *postmodernity*. But the term remains valuable exactly because it carries ambiguous freight. It claims only that we
live after modernity and its unchallenged faith in secular reason. To
return one last time to our proverbial jet airplane: Postmodernity is a
signpost letting us know that we have flown to the borders of modernity,
even if it does not tell us precisely what lies beyond those borders.

But postmodernity can serve as more than another name for nowhere.
Postmodern thinkers are often preoccupied with certain themes that will

provide benchmarks as I try to locate the privileges and responsibilities of Christian family in our time and place.

1. *The postmodern world is a world which has lost its supposed universals and common goods.* The gods, as I have already said, now compete openly. We must not take a cavalier attitude toward this state of affairs—our times are too dangerous for that—but it does present some advantages to Christians. Now that there can no longer be simple, final appeals to "objective," "secular" or "neutral" reason, Christians need not be ashamed of appealing to reasons based on the particular story of Israel and Jesus. Thus I will not assume that a Christian ethic of fidelity, for instance, must be stated in supposedly neutral, nonbiblical terms that would self-evidently make sense to "any" sane person. I will not pretend that the Christian suspicion of sex outside marriage is vindicated by practical, secular appeals to how "happy" or "healthy" people are if they save their virginity until marriage. (The whole point is, what is true happiness, what is authentic health? And the answers depend on what story actually reveals truth and reality.) Ironically, the postmodern situation frees the Christian family to be Christian, to live distinctively and unabashedly out of its particular story.

2. *The postmodern world is a fragmented world, more and more populated with isolated and drifting individuals.* As we have noted, the common Western framework of values about marriage, divorce, acceptable popular entertainment and so forth has broken down. In an even more general sense, people no longer feel bound by the authority of any one community consensus. We live in an age of hyperindividualism.

But the Christian account, like Aristotle's, sees human beings as fundamentally social animals. The untethered individual, drifting without any sense of place, belonging or responsibility to a larger purpose, can establish no deep and satisfactory identity. People searching for an identity will be attracted to a community that has some sense of where it has come from and where it is going. People trying to incarnate Christian family in a more and more boldly post-Christian world will realize the necessity of journeying with others who see with the same eyes. So in the pages that follow I will emphasize the centrality of the church as the one and only Christian polity in the world. It is the true basis and hope and support of the Christian nuclear family. I mean this in conscious opposition to both spiritualized individualism ("my religion is between God and me") and the strategy of saving the Christian family by restoring one's nation-state to a quasi-Christian status.

3. *The postmodern world is a world acutely aware of the "other" or stranger.* Postmodernists, as we have seen, are suspicious of the assumption that any argument or way of life can come from beyond culture, that it can exist purely apart from any particular time and place. Ours is a time in which many new approaches to theology arise, from Latinos, Africans, Koreans and others who suspect the way white Europeans have written theology has definitely been influenced by the fact that they were white Europeans. Likewise, psychologists such as Carol Gilligan have shown that women make moral decisions in a way different from men; popular writer Deborah Tannen suggests that male-female relations should be viewed as a form of crosscultural communication. In a time of failed consensus, cultural transition and high-gear individualism, we are vividly aware that people are different. So I will be concerned with the Christian family's ability to relate to strangers— especially when those strangers are their own children.

In Search of an Ark

All told, the postmodern world is a world of flux, change, uncertainty. In that sense, it is an awkward world for the family. After all, no matter how well adults adapt to constant change, children remain the consummate conservatives. To grow up healthy, trustful, secure, they demand stability in their formative years.

For this reason, if for no other, we want and wish family to be a still point in the turning world. Yet I have said family takes many forms and changes over time. Is there, then, any place for us to stand, any secure place for our children? Rudely dumped into the raging white water of postmodernity, we turn now to search for some footing. In a world whose sufferings and limitations Christians are meant to share, our hope is not to be impervious to the water, forever dry and utterly safe. Instead, our truest and best hope is to find an ark—an ark with a rudder and so a sense of direction, an ark whose passengers have a sure star by which to navigate.

CHAPTER TWO

THE UNNATURALNESS
OF FAMILY

•

From there to here,
from here to there,
funny things
are everywhere.

Dr. Seuss, *One Fish, Two Fish,
Red Fish, Blue Fish*

In the mid-nineteenth century, a young English traveler ventured into
the gorilla country of West Africa. Accompanied by a few African
guides, Winwood Reade trod where no white had trod before. For a time
he sojourned with the Rembo tribesfolk. Among them he found the
stunning Ananga, daughter of the Rembo king. Reade was smitten with
her hands ("full and finely moulded"), her feet ("exquisitely small"),
her complexion ("a deep warm colour") and her eyes ("large and filled
with a melancholy expression").

The intrepid Englishman had gone to Africa to observe the gorilla in
its natural habitat. But Ananga presented a more appealing study. So
for weeks Reade relished her company daily. He delighted in her
"fluttering eyes" and her "poor little heart, which used to throb so loudly
when we were alone." Eventually, of course, he seized the moment and

kissed the king's daughter squarely on her lips. To his surprise, Ananga screamed and "bounded from the house like a frightened fawn." Swooningly infatuated, Reade had forgotten that

this mode of salutation is utterly unknown in Western Africa. Ananga knew that the serpent moistens its victim with its lips before it begins its repast. All the tales of white cannibals which she had heard from infancy had returned to her. The poor child had thought that I was going to dine off her, and she had run for her life!

The Family and the Ozone Layer

From Reade's standpoint, he could have done nothing more natural than kiss the princess. When Westerners are sexually attracted, we kiss. But given the princess's reaction, just how "natural" was his impulse? After all, the Rembo were not alone in their aversion to kissing. New Zealand Maoris, Australian aborigines, South Sea islanders and the Alaskan Eskimos were ignorant of kissing until white traders, explorers and missionaries taught them the technique. The Chinese have also considered kissing revoltingly reminiscent of cannibalism. And all of Africa, in Reade's own ethnocentric terms, once had "the sad distinction of being the largest non-kissing area in the world."

If we mean by *natural* something that is universal and biologically determined, kissing is not natural. In fact, many more important aspects of sexuality are not in this sense natural. Sexual expression, even sexual orientation, has varied greatly across time and cultures. But to admit this is disturbing. Sexuality is so basic to our identities that we hate to see it as something unstable, plastic and vulnerable to change.

Similarly, it's not easy to allow that the family has taken many shapes and forms across time and cultures. Unless we grow up as orphans in an institution, each of us is born or adopted into a nuclear family. Family defines us, leaving its imprint on every aspect of our character. It is the earliest and most indelible "world" we know. In it we learn to trust or distrust life, the universe, God. Because family is so basic to who we are, we yearn for it to be an unchanging bulwark against personal and societal chaos. It is the ground we stand on. No wonder we want to call it natural and believe it to be as final and invulnerable as the force of gravity.

And since family is so basic and foundational, we may not be eager to reflect on how much it differs from place to place and time to time. It is not convenient to know the Greeks considered homosexuality natural, presenting little or no problem for their families. We do not like to be reminded that many families, including biblical ones, found polygamy as natural as monogamy. Yet our world, the postmodern world, has become increasingly aware of how much culture shapes family. We live in a society divided over how family should be defined. Do we best understand family as a man, a woman and their biological (or adopted) offspring? Or is society better off if we widen the definition of family to include two men or two women living together, with or without children? Is lifelong fidelity, heterosexual or homosexual, at all realistic or even ideal? However marriage is defined, why do married people have children? How many children should they have? In a world of burdened resources, *should* they have children?

The difference between us and Winwood Reade is that he had to leave home and travel thousands of miles to realize how unnatural kissing is. And I suspect that once he had settled back in England a few weeks, kissing was every bit as secure a feature of his cosmos as before Ananga. But the postmodern world is an intensely pluralistic world. The Rembo and their ways have come to our doorstep. We have friends, employers and coworkers who would define family differently from the way we do. In fact, we go to church with people who define it differently. If we forget this for an evening or a weekend, the television or newspaper or a Sunday-school argument brings the reality right back home.

We may still affirm that a specific definition of family is the true and natural one, but even this certitude is more like the ozone layer than the force of gravity. It may really be there, and our well-being may ultimately depend on it, but it will not prosper by itself. A particular form of family, like the ozone layer, can be damaged or destroyed. It is something we must fight for, something we must "save" (as the National Association of Evangelicals declared at its 1982 annual convention).

Perhaps because this state of affairs is so unsettling, we often insist that our definition of family is the natural one in the strongest sense: more like the force of gravity than the ozone layer. We want to believe that our "family" is obviously superior and that those who deny it are as foolish and perverse as antigravity know-nothings who step off a cliff in obedience to their misplaced faith. In this light, much of the early Christian response to the AIDS epidemic was the equivalent of saying, "We told you there were consequences. You knew it yourselves. Anybody who would walk off the side of a mountain deserves to lie in a broken heap at the bottom."

Yet I do not think we will help the family or further the mission of the church unless we recognize our situation for what it is. The postmodern world is a confused and divided world. We war in our hearts and public squares over many essentials, and one of them is the family. So, although it may be disconcerting, I am going to dwell on the "unnaturalness" of the family in some detail. It is only after we have admitted the family takes many shapes and forms that we can seriously ask what a *Christian* shape and form is, and dream about how we can better embody it here and now.

The Family: The Bourgeois Model
In chapter one I said that what some evangelicals call the traditional

family is actually only two centuries old. It is, in fact, the nineteenth-century bourgeois family. Now, for the sake of showing that family takes different shapes in different cultures, I want to elaborate on that claim. In *The War over the Family,* Brigitte and Peter Berger sympathetically describe six characteristics of the bourgeois family. Here I want to briefly survey each of these characteristics and show that each represents an aspect of the evangelical "traditional family."

1. Family life is eminently attractive and the home, as a private refuge from the harsh public world, is a major focus of life. Clearly, as we saw in chapter one, the importance of the home is one of the preeminent values of the evangelical subculture. Evangelicals have also understood the home as shelter from public life. Typical are statements such as writer Rus Walton's: "In such times as these . . . the Christian home should be a holy refuge." In the same book, *One Nation Under God,* Walton declares the home a "Christian oasis" and "an island of serenity . . . in a hectic, plastic, often avaricious world."

2. There is a heightened concern for children, particularly for their formation and education. Many religious traditions have imagined sanctity and fulfillment separate from children. Eastern faiths, for instance, expect the individual to turn inward for a glimpse of highest reality. The Christian monastic tradition envisions sanctity apart from the birthing and rearing of children. But in the evangelical subculture, religious life concentrates on family and children. So pastor Kenneth Chafin declares:

The one experience which will give meaning to all the others is:

Love God.

Love yourself.

Love your mate.

Love your children.

Much of the evangelical concern for children focuses on their development. Consequently there are prominent debates about the adequacy of public schools. Books on home-schooling, and discipline in general, are popular.

Thus, though attitudes toward children are shifting in our culture, evangelicals strongly expect normal persons to marry, bear children and make family "the one experience that will give meaning to all the others." (What mission and hope would Pastor Chafin promise the single people in his congregation, those who have not secured mates or begotten children?) It is assumed that parents will naturally, intensely love their children and want to devote time and attention to their development.

3. Family is the source of personal values and identity for both sexes. I have already emphasized that evangelicals invest tremendous spiritual and moral importance in the family. James Dobson, to add another example, expects husbands and fathers to place "their wives and children at the highest level in their system of priorities."

For traditionalist evangelicals, sharper male and female identity is provided by the assignment of hierarchical sexual roles. Strikingly, traditionalist books on the family are again and again structured along the line of patriarchal hierarchy. The middle three chapters of Kenneth Chafin's book, for instance, are titled "Fathers Are Important," "Mothers Are Essential" and "Listen to the Children." Two-thirds of Larry Christenson's *The Christian Family* concerns "God's Order" for "Mates," "Wives," "Husbands," "Children" and "Parents." Likewise, Gene Getz's *The Measure of a Family* devotes chapters to "The Christian Wife—and Submission," "The Christian Husband—and Headship" and "Christian Children—and Obedience."

For the female, then, motherhood and the role of submissive wife are reaffirmed as the noblest aspirations available to woman. The male, or *Total Man,* as one title has it, should provide for, love and lead his family. The traditionalist locates the source of identity and values squarely in the bosom of the bourgeois family.

4. *Romantic love is the major motive for marriage.* Evangelical traditionalists, however traditional they may be, do not expect marriages to be arranged by parents or to be decided on the basis of wealth and social status. Traditionalists, like the rest of our culture, expect people to choose their mates on the basis of romantic attraction. So there are evangelical books on dating, even some offering tips on how to lure an attractive man *(Not Just Any Man: A Practical Guide to Finding Mr. Right).* Christian musical artists pepper their albums with paeans to romantic love; several publishers produce Christian romance novels. Christian counselors now write and speak explicitly about the enjoyment of sex within marriage. They encourage a variety of sexual positions and techniques, provided that both mates consent.

5. *Spouses are intensely affectionate and respectful to one another.* This point follows naturally enough from the others. If family is the focus of the good life, if it is viewed as a haven and solace, and if romantic love is its springboard, spouses will be expected to be intensely affectionate and respectful. The bourgeois and traditionalist evangelical expectations of family are extraordinarily high. Indeed, I do not think sociologist James Davison Hunter overstates the case in calling these expectations "utopian" and "Edenic." In this version of family, sentiment occupies center stage.

6. *The woman is paramount in the home, which is her special domain.* Traditionalist evangelical Michael Brown speaks for many when he reaffirms "motherhood [as] among the highest and most noble roles to which a woman can aspire" and "the privilege of caring for children . . . as a fulfilling and rewarding task."

On this point, notice a curiosity. Our traditional family makes women the religious exemplars of the household. True enough, evangelical traditionalists insist that the husband and father is the religious leader of the family. But they have also adopted the nineteenth-century idealization of femininity and domesticity. Protestant preachers of that era admired the piety of women and held them up as models of godliness. The observant French visitor Alexis de Tocqueville saw the American woman as the "protector of morals." Traditionalists evidence similar attitudes today when they coach women to devote their energies to the home and extol the power of the "hand that rocks the cradle."

All this is especially intriguing when we remember that, in much of Christian tradition and history, women were seen as seductresses. Eve, of course, was long interpreted as the cause of the Fall, dragging an innocent Adam down after her. Women were potent lures to evil and so were literally in need of taming or *domestication*. But contemporary evangelical traditionalists, influenced by a nineteenth-century model of the family, have stood this image on its head. The seductress has become religious and moral exemplar.

For instance, some traditionalists applaud the arguments of social critic George Gilder. Gilder depicts men, not women, as sexually anarchic creatures who, for the good of society, must be tamed within family. There they will be anchored by women (whom Gilder considers more sexually stable) and by the responsibilities of fatherhood. So traditionalists long for golden days when a woman devoted all her energies to the household and nurtured the spiritual welfare of the family.

The "Unbiblical" Israelite Family

These are the characteristics of the bourgeois family outlined by Peter and Brigitte Berger and enthusiastically adopted by many evangelicals. The Bergers, while quite sympathetic to the bourgeois family, are clear that it is a form of family that crystallized in the nineteenth century. But the evangelicals who call this the "traditional" and often the "biblical" family are not so clear on its comparatively late historical provenance. In fact, if this is the biblical family, the families of the Old Testament were unbiblical. Several characteristics of the Hebrew family radically set it apart from our bourgeois or traditional family.

One of the most obvious differences is that, unlike the bourgeois family, the Israelite family could be polygamous. But polygamy was mainly confined to the wealthier Israelites, and to the earlier periods of Israel's history. Several Old Testament evidences show that Israel markedly tended toward monogamous marriage.

A more fundamental difference with bourgeois family was that Israelites simply did not sharply divide the private and public worlds, as does a bourgeois vision of the family. Ancient Israel had no centralized, industrial economy, so households provided their own economic wherewithal. Agricultural households, such as Gideon's (Judg 6), grew grain and fruit, and grazed sheep, goats and a few cattle. Seminomadic or pastoral households, such as Nabal's (1 Sam 25), bred herds of sheep and goats, probably practiced some agriculture and bartered for the remainder of their foodstuffs. Thus neither father nor mother left the "private" world to go earn the family's bread in the "public."

The Old Testament household was less narrow or circumscribed than ours in other ways. The U.S. Census Bureau tells us the average American household, for example, consists of 2.63 people. The average Hebrew household numbered closer to 50 or 100 people. (Jacob's, we are told, consisted of 66 [Gen 46:26].) The Israelites had no real conception of a nuclear family. What we call the nuclear family they saw seamlessly woven into the multigenerational extended family. Every family centered on a patriarch. Each son, with his wife, children and (in some cases) servants, lived in a separate shelter. So a Hebrew household or family would actually be a small village consisting of

several adjacent buildings. What's more, these households would sometimes induct and include as members of the family aliens or sojourners
who had permanently taken shelter with them. So Judges 17:12 speaks
of a sojourning Levite being "installed" in the house of Micah.

Israel's family, then, was quite unlike the bourgeois family. Ours is
a highly atomized and mobile society in which individuals or nuclear
families routinely dwell apart from relatives and, in a pinch, can rely
on the ministrations of the welfare state. By contrast, Hebrew nuclear
families were located within a larger "house." These houses in turn were
united by marriage and kinship to form clans (as in Josh 7:17); several
clans then constituted a tribe; and the confederation of tribes made up
Israel. Houses, clans or tribes were counted on for mutual aid, to supply
male heirs, keep or recover land, rescue members from debt slavery and
avenge murder. Outside such ties, the individual was vulnerable to
violence or theft, since the perpetrator would have no need to fear
punishment. So Hagar, in Genesis 21, has plenty of reason to mourn.
Cast out of Abraham's house, abandoned in the wilderness without
family ties and protection, she is as good as dead. In other words,
matters of law and justice were as much a private (or family) concern
as a public concern. In fact, there was no such distinction.

There is another pervasive difference between the bourgeois and Old
Testament families. Stripped of economic and political functions, the
bourgeois family concentrates on the only thing left to it: affection.
Spouses and children are supposed to adore the company of family.
And, as already noted, our expectations of family warmth are often
stretched to the point of being utopian. We can rather easily sentimentalize family and imagine it to be something far rosier than anything we
actually experience.

By contrast, the Israelite conception of family could hardly be called
sentimental. This is not to say affection never existed in Old Testament

families. But often it did not, and it was never seen as key. It is worth remembering that Israelite marriages were not romantically based. They were arranged. Marriage represented a covenant not merely between two individuals, but between two families. *Mohar,* or a "bride price," was offered by the groom's family to seal the covenant between his and the bride's family, to establish the prestige of the husband and his family, and to transfer to the husband authority over the woman in question (see, for instance, Gen 34; 1 Sam 18:25; Lev 27).

In short, marriages were arranged—usually by the fathers—to consolidate the strength and resources of the families involved. Scholar John Bright believes that behind David's demand for the return of Michal, Saul's daughter and David's estranged wife, was "certainly the hope that a male issue would unite the claims of his house and Saul's." And Caleb offers his daughter to "whoever attacks Kiriath-sepher and takes it," baldly making marriage serve his political and military objectives (Josh 15:16).

Further evidence of the unsentimental quality of Israelite family is the Old Testament's matter-of-fact depiction of the father's complete control over the disposal of his children. Abraham could sacrifice Isaac (Gen 22). Jephthah apparently sacrificed his daughter (Judg 11:34-40). If "your own son or daughter" entices the father to serve another god, "your own hand shall be first against them to execute them" (Deut 13:6-9). A father could sell his daughter into slavery, even concubinage (Ex 21:7-11) or prostitution (Lev 19:29). He could have a disobedient son stoned (Deut 21:12-21) or an errant daughter burned (Gen 38:24).

Again, I am not pretending that affection never existed in Israelite families. Far from it. Jacob, after all, worked a total of fourteen years to win Rachel (Gen 29). Elkanah attempted to comfort the barren Hannah by tenderly declaring their love: "Am I not more to you than ten sons?" (1 Sam 1:8). The story of David and Michal shows them

falling in (and out) of love, and depicts the heartbreaking affection of
Michal's second husband for her (1 Sam 18, 25; 2 Sam 3). Isaac and
Rebecca learned to love one another after she was delivered to him from
afar (Gen 24). In more general terms, affection for spouses is evident
in laws that attempt to sort out just deserts in cases where a polygamous
husband loves one wife more than the other (Deut 21:15). Proverbs
30:21-23 declares that the earth trembles when "an unloved woman . . .
gets a husband." Ecclesiastes 9:9 advises, "Enjoy life with the wife
whom you love." Of course, and supremely, there is the passionate Song
of Songs. Israelite marriages could obviously be affectionate.

Just the same, we do well not to sentimentalize the Old Testament
family and imagine that its relations were suffused with the sort of
affection that has come to be expected today. If the companionship
sought in contemporary Western marriages was possible then, it was
not seen as the central good or purpose of marriage. The arranged
marriages of the Israelites were much more consciously and directly
undertaken for economic, political and social purposes. Polygamy,
concubinage and inheritance rights contributed to severe rivalries and
tensions right at the heart of the family.

There is conflict between Sarah and Hagar, Rachel and Leah, Hannah
and Peninnah. Jacob tricks his father into giving him his brother Esau's
rightful blessing (Gen 27). Noah is mocked by his son Ham (Gen
9:20-26), and Lot is intoxicated by his daughters, who then lie with him
(Gen 19:32). David's entire story is rife with family tension: his on-
again, off-again relationship with Michal; his scandalous and painful
union with Bathsheba; the raping of Tamar by a son, Amnon; and
(largely as a result) son Absalom's rebellion against David—a rebellion
ending in palace intrigue, with Solomon and David's other sons vio-
lently jockeying to inherit his throne (1 and 2 Sam).

This list could be extended to include the original sibling rivalry of

Cain and Abel (Gen 4), Joseph's dispensation into slavery at the hands of his brothers (Gen 37:25-28) and other incidents. So, in sum, there could be and was affection in the Israelite family. But overall, in the words of scholar Thomas Martin, "while the family was of key importance for the whole fabric of Israelite society and was the principal aim of individuals, the domestic setting is not pictured as primarily a loving supportive group."

If We Did What Came Naturally, Would There Be Families?

This brief tour through the family museum of Israel underlines my contention that, historically, the family has taken different shapes and forms. It demonstrates that a particular model of family does not just fall into place all by itself. Like the museum exhibit, a family form is arranged. It is erected for certain purposes, with careful intention and not a little energy.

We tend to think of museums as deathly boring. But they are not boring in at least one respect. With the relics of bygone eras—the busts of emperors, the swords of soldiers, the finery of court ladies—museums remind us that entire civilizations fall as surely as they rise. It sobers us to realize our civilization is not exempt. There will be a *last* American president, a last British or Australian prime minister, just as there was a last Israelite king. And there will be a *last* traditional family, just as there was a last Israelite family. So wandering into a museum can be an unhappy experience. The Israelite museum raises its own disturbing questions: Just how insecure is family? What do its many and shifting forms mean? Is anything about family natural and unchanging?

Anthropologists study a great variety of cultures and assure us that there are three constants about family.

All animals, including humans, ordinarily possess sexual drives. Obviously the sex drive is important for procreation, which enables

society and the human race to last more than one generation. But with
the sex drive also comes sexual competition. Particular men and women
desire other particular men and women—the strongest, the most beautiful, the most intelligent, the wealthiest and so on. If sexual competition is not contained, a society's members will constantly war with one
another. And sexual competition is naturally contained by marriage,
which marks off particular mates and removes them to a nonwar zone.
To avoid overwhelming sexual warfare, all societies develop some form
of marriage. It may mean a woman can marry several men, or a man can
marry several women, or both; it may mean monogamy; it may mean
something else again. Marriage takes different shapes. In this sense it
is a human contrivance, but humans in all times and places contrive it.
So we can say marriage is natural for people.

Anthropologists report a second point. Untended, the human offspring won't survive long outside the womb. It will in fact be dependent
for several years. And the more complicated a society, the more training
a child will need to be successfully introduced into it. Family arrangements—particular parents with particular children—have proved the
most efficient way to reproduce and rear children. As with marriage,
family arrangements take many forms. Sometimes the newly married
move in with the wife's parents, sometimes with the husband's. Sometimes the newly married establish a home apart. In our day we are
experimenting with families run by a single parent, the father or the
mother alone. But somehow or other, dependent children must be
tended and socialized. They need plenty of attention, consistently
given, by a few designated persons. So we can say parenting is natural
for people.

Finally, anthropologists see a third enduring reality. Men and women
are different. Behind anatomy itself there are few constants for saying
exactly how, and how much, we are different. But we are clearly

different. Marriage and family structures help us deal with our differences. They provide a complementary division of roles, labor and goods between the sexes. Nowadays we are sharply aware of how much such divisions can vary from culture to culture. Feminism, among other things, has sensitized us to the fact that men in all cultures didn't earn the family's living. True, in most cases men have lorded it over women. But in some cultures men lorded idly while women gathered food, sewed clothing, shepherded children and otherwise sustained the family.

Our culture is in the middle of a debate about exactly how the roles of women and men should complement each other, and whether this complementarity demands the subordination of one sex to another. For a while some talked of androgyny and the potential blurring or even elimination of differences between the sexes. But acute feminist thinkers soon noticed that androgyny tended to take a peculiarly masculine form. Women were striving to be as aggressive and detached as men, and so in a sense wishing to become men. In response, these feminists developed a subtler recognition that there are "women's ways of knowing" and behaving, and that these should be affirmed on their own terms. More recently "men's studies" have developed, and avant-garde males retreat for weekends of exploring the meaning of masculinity. It is both a confusing and an exciting time. Women and men are seeking to better understand and appreciate our differences. But with all the flux, it appears we can still say that some division of roles, goods and labor between the sexes is natural. This, too, occurs in all times and places.

Naturally, but Not Instinctually

Drawing on anthropologists, then, I want to affirm that there are three broad ways in which family is natural: it serves (1) to sanction and regulate sexual mating; (2) to enable the reproduction, survival and socialization of children; and (3) to apportion roles, labor and goods between the sexes.

But as should be clear by now, *natural* is a tricky word. It sounds like *nature,* and when we think of nature we think of trees, the sky, rocks and various animals. Trees, skies, rocks—these are utterly predictable. A tree's roots always grope toward water; rocks always smash through windows when thrown at them. Animals are not so predictable. The mole can burrow toward or away from water; toss a bird at a window and it may turn and fly the other direction. But still, if we study animals long enough, we can confidently predict their behavior in response to given conditions. This is because animals depend so much on instinct, or biological programming.

Biological programming makes animal families quite predictable. Black widow families always end up single-parent families, since the female devours the male after mating. Geese families are always more stable than black widow families, since geese mate for life and neither male nor female consumes its mate. Tolstoy may or may not have been right about all happy (human) families being alike, but instinct means that all animal families, within their species, are alike.

People make for much more complicated family portraits. Culture, or human contrivance and values, is fundamentally at work even in our three natural aspects of family. And culture looms even larger when we look *in detail* at the form and content of actual families. Who will marry whom, and how many persons may he or she marry? Which sort of people will be forbidden as candidates for marriage? Is it honorable, dishonorable or indifferent not to marry? How many children ought a family to include, and will these children live with their biological mothers or fathers or both? What roles and labor will males and females adopt? How will goods be inherited and passed down through the family? All these and many more questions are answered differently from culture to culture.

This is the case because instinct, if we possess it at all, plays a much lesser role in human society than in the animal kingdom. Animals develop essential instinctual, biological equipment within the womb. They arrive in the outside world needing only to develop tools already possessed, to perfect inborn techniques. So salmon do not need to teach their young to swim upstream each mating season. Ducks need not guide their offspring along the migratory route.

People, by comparison, are instinctually underdeveloped. Many of our essential tools for surviving in the outside world do not exist even in a nascent form within the womb. Babies are not born, for instance, with the knowledge of how to light a fire. Our tools for survival are introduced and developed outside the womb, when the human infant is not only *in* the outside world but already relating to it in many complex ways. The process of becoming maturely human happens as we interact with the environment. And the developing person becomes a mature person not only within a particular natural environment, but within a particular social and cultural order as well. My cat, Tobermory, would be pretty much the same cat if he had been born and reared in Alaska rather than Illinois. But I would have been a quite different person had I been born and reared in New York rather than Oklahoma.

Culture is crucial in forming our sexual attractions, even our appetite for particular kinds of food. Culture can make bisexuality "normal"; culture determines whether people salivate or grow nauseated when they smell *kim chee* (Korean cabbage, fermented). Thus culture molds and channels our most basic physiological responses. Even the age at which menstruation sets in for girls varies with cultural factors.

All this decisively sets us apart from animals. Animals are, for the most part, biologically programmed. To the degree people are programmed at all, we are culturally programmed. Without culture, as anthropologist Clifford Geertz writes, our "behavior would be virtually ungovernable, a mere chaos of pointless acts and exploding emotions." So culture "is not just an ornament of human existence but . . . an essential condition for it." There is, he continues, "no such thing as human nature independent of culture." We are born incomplete creatures "who complete themselves through culture."

Human "nature," then, is much more complex than animal "nature." We must recognize that the naturalness of human family is not the naturalness of the animal family. The naturalness of the animal family derives (for the most part) from *biological necessity*. The naturalness of the human family derives (for the most part) from *social necessity*. Animals form families, and particular sorts of families, because something "in their blood" tells them to. We form families, and particular sorts of families, because our parents and our church and our nation tell us to. And they in turn tell us to form particular sorts of families because they have come to believe those kinds of families best serve the family line, the mission of the kingdom or the survival of the state.

The burden of this book grows from a postmodern recognition of this sometimes exhilarating, sometimes vexatious reality. In the postmodern world, people argue over which kind of family should be "saved," ensconced in the law, supported by taxation policies, reinforced by television programs and movies. And in a postmodern world, the church and the state often find their goals in competition. They do not always agree about the shape the family should take, the destiny it should fulfill. Since for people what is natural is a matter of social necessity, church and nation may hold different notions of what is or should be the natural family.

For Christians this is no surprise. We in fact expect that families and states will not even know what is ultimately good or natural for them unless, in the life of the church, they hear and see the story of the kingdom come. Our confession is that the good and the true are revealed through the particular story of Israel and Jesus Christ. So we cannot understand family apart from our confession, which is our story. We must resort explicitly to that story to "explain" family and our hopes for family.

Of Seuss and the Kingdom

To summarize the pilgrimage of this chapter, I am claiming that we must sharpen our awareness of the different meanings of the word *natural* as it applies to family. And I am claiming that as Christians we affirm that all that is true and real about family is finally revealed in Jesus Christ and the kingdom he inaugurated. Exactly what, then, are we Christians affirming about ourselves, about the world and about the family?

We are affirming first of all that God created everything that is, the world of people and the world of animals. For people, not just for animals, there is a God-given order and structure that, if heeded, best serves our health and welfare. Certain broad aspects of this carry across all cultures (for instance, the need to regulate sexuality and somehow or other parent the young). But other important, more particular aspects do not.

This is the case because what Christians call the Fall has obscured our knowledge of creation and God's ordering of it. Given the Fall, what is good or natural for the family is not self-evident. People in fact strongly disagree about what is the natural family. Christians affirm that only through God's revelation—through the particular culture of Israel, in the particular person of Jesus—can we see the natural order as it really is and as it ought to be. This is the crux of Paul's argument in Romans 1 and 2. In our fallenness we are given up to a corrupted imagination, to senseless, darkened, debased minds (1:21, 28). In ignorance and self-deception, we deny and corrode our true nature. This results in no less than the degradation of our bodies and the fracturing of all our social relations—including the family (1:24-32).

Because of the Fall, the early chapters of Genesis do not tell us all we need to know, or even what is most crucial for us to know, for the formation of the good and natural family. Our object is not merely to restore family as it was in Eden, before the Fall. The Fall means that family life was interrupted before it matured or ripened to its potential, before it fulfilled its destiny. With family life as with all life, this fulfillment will not come until history's end, when God will transform heaven and earth. Yet the pivotal point in history has already occurred, with the coming of Jesus and his initiation of the kingdom. In the career and death of Jesus, the world has already been reconciled to God.

So all people are now marked by Christ and live in the time between the times—between the time of kingdom's initiation and the time of its fulfillment. The church is the particular people called to witness to and live true to this reality. That the kingdom has come, that the world really has been changed, is the most basic of realities, but is still denied or ignored (even by those in the church) much of the time. We often fail to see what is best for ourselves and for the world, "but we do see Jesus" (Heb 2:9). Only by seeing Jesus and all that he means can we begin to build natural families, families that serve the one and final reality, which we call the kingdom of God.

With this understanding, this vision of what is real and true, we cannot affirm that the hope of the world rests in the bosom of the biological or nuclear family. And against Abraham Lincoln, we cannot affirm that America is the "last, best hope" of the world. The hope of the world is Jesus Christ, and the people called to bear witness to that hope is a people drawn from all families and all nations. It is the church.

Let me put it in terms I used earlier. At the end of chapter one I said our best and truest hope in these tumultuous times is an ark—an ark with a sense of direction and a sure star by which to navigate. The church is that ark. And the star, of course, is Jesus Christ.

Restoring and redeeming the family, then, does not begin with the nation or with the family itself. It begins with the church. It begins with a church that recognizes the wisdom of Dr. Seuss:

There and here,

Here and there,

Funny things are everywhere.

God created us as complicated creatures who complete ourselves in culture. Funny things *are* everywhere. No culture is as "natural" as it pretends. Fashions change: in clothes, we wonder just twenty years later how polka-dot neckties and red Naugahyde miniskirts were ever taken seriously. In more fundamental matters, such as parenting and what makes for a true marriage, the differences and changes aren't so obvious. But they are there.

When the church realizes that funny things are everywhere, it can ask what peculiar shape its family should take in particular times and places. It will no longer assume that what its host culture asks of its family is as natural as rain. It will notice what sorts of funny things its host culture expects of family. And it will see just how unfunny some of these expectations actually are.

Such a realization, I am sure, is the need of the church and its family in every place and every time. For reasons I now hope to make clear, it is certainly the need of the church and its family in the post-Christian West, in these the latter years of the twentieth century.

CHAPTER THREE

ADVANCED CAPITALISM
& THE LOST ART
OF CHRISTIAN FAMILY

●

[Money and the market] is the center of their existence.
. . . The green numbers on the board. This is . . . their way
of continuing on through rotting flesh, their closest
taste of immortality. . . . "Financiers are more spiritually
advanced than monks on an island."
Don DeLillo, *Players*

For years she'd heard people saying, all sorts, really, here
and there: "Do whatever you want as long as nobody gets
hurt." They said: "As long as both parties agree, do it,
whatever." They said: "Whatever feels right, as long as
you both want to do it and nobody gets hurt, there's no
reason not to do it." They said: "As long as there's mutual
agreement and the right feeling, no matter what or who."
Don DeLillo, *Players*

"Actually I'm living with a Vietnamese girl," I said.
"Marriage is a lost art."
Don DeLillo, *Americana*

My wife, Sandy, and I have lived for most of our marriage in
suburban Chicago. In one nearby suburb, the average home is occupied
by the same owner less than two years. When we bought our current
home, our realtor admired the new roof and commented that by the time

it needed replacement, we would (statistically speaking) be in our second different home.

Here life is emphatically not of one piece. We work with one set of people and pray with another. We shop and play in an assortment of neighborhoods and communities. It is hard to know or be known. Friendship, so natural in the small town where we both grew up, must be pursued with intentionality and discipline. And even then, it may soon face the added challenge of distance: within the last five years, three of my closest friends have moved across the country.

Certainly our little family gets support. But extended family is available only by phone and occasional visits. Other support must come from vital if makeshift communities, an erratic constellation of friends careening in and out of our orbit.

The keynote, then, is not fidelity or roots or a sense of place. If the image of small-town life is a sturdy, intricately rooted tree, the image of suburban life is the hydroponic plant that floats on the water's surface and easily adapts when moved to another pond or tank. Rather than supporting and maintaining the richness and stability of a single, personal community, suburbanites often have little attachment to the "bedroom" towns where they reside and pay taxes. For closeness and support, suburbanites must attempt to maintain several more informal communities, often voluntary associations formed around common interests such as biking, sailing, photography, literature—or worshiping God.

We have a greater variety of relationships than small-town dwellers, but these relationships also tend to be short-term and focus on only one or two dimensions of our lives. So it is extremely difficult for these relationships not to be shallower, not to float on the surface of our lives rather than sink roots into the depths of a shared soil.

In these more informal, limited, briefer and shallower relationships, fundamental life-commitments—such as baptismal vows, marriage and family—are easily not central. What is central is the common interest friends happen to share on one or a few points. And these more tenuous relationships make it hard to seriously assist one another in honoring baptismal or marriage vows. If I play racquetball with you once a week or sit in your reading group once a month, what business is it of yours if I cheat on my wife?

More significantly, the hydroponic plant becomes the model not just for friendships but for all my relationships—including the family. I certainly share some interests with my wife, but in contemporary suburbia a lifetime commitment seems rash. Consider how much I and she will change over a lifetime. A lifetime commitment could be unduly binding, preventing either or both of us from becoming all we might be. And children, of course, infamously "tie parents down," making it harder to move to a new, more promising pond.

Now life in postmodern urban and suburban society is in many respects invigorating. For instance, living in such a kaleidoscopic setting means that I am less likely to simply (and perhaps irresponsibly) assume the self presented to me by the more stable and coherent small-town environment. In suburbia I am very much aware of a respon-sibility for the kind of character I develop, the kind of person I will become, since nearly every day I face the flesh-and-blood challenge of people who strive to become different kinds of persons. Yet the truth remains: my environment does not encourage lifelong marriage or enduring family.

The challenge facing the church and Christian family in the contem-porary West can be helpfully put in exactly these terms. How can we really be the *community* of Christ-followers in a setting that pushes us toward understanding our commitment to God as a mere personal interest, a private concern akin to a preference of tennis over golf? How do we redefine our situation on more fundamentally biblical terms—where Jesus is Lord of the cosmos and not merely of some individuals' private lives—and begin to live in that light? How can we maintain the fidelity and long-term commitments of Christian family in an environment that increasingly encourages novelty and short-term commitment?

Surely an important first step is understanding what created and fuels these particular cultural challenges. We need to understand our postmodern world, with its vast array of choices, in more detail. What, really, are the church and Christian family up against?

What Really Ails the Family

If asked what most threatens family today, Christian family advocates present a list commonly including pornography, drugs, public schools and secular humanism. I agree that such factors challenge and can hinder Christian family. But two things bother me about the accepted list of enemies to the family.

First, the list lets Christians off the hook. It shoves the real enemies of our family outside our camp. True, to some degree pornography, drugs and so forth have invaded our ranks. But few of us read *Playboy* regularly if at all, and even at the terrible peak of the drug crisis, only a fraction of all adults and teens were actually using hard drugs. Yet our divorce rates are high—among American Christians these rates very nearly match the national average. Some experts contend that child abuse is more common in our homes than in the larger society. Clearly, Christian families are hurting. And whatever is tearing us apart is *among us*. It is not simply—or even primarily—something secular humanists thrust at us from the darkness beyond the rosy glow of our campfire.

This points up the second shortcoming of the common list. It does not go deep enough. It fails to ask what it is about our setting and ourselves that so inclines us to eroding families. It fails to look critically at the suburban lifestyle it often embraces. It fails to consider what may underlie pornography or drug use *and* the failure of Christian family.

So what is the deeper problem? To put it bluntly, the deeper problem is that capitalism has succeeded. It has succeeded for good, certainly. Capitalism has given us a more materially prosperous world, fostered creativity and given us a wide array of desirable choices, so any criticism of it demands some nuance. But capitalism has also succeeded for ill.

I am not suggesting Christians should oppose free markets. In terms of morality as well as efficiency, forms of a mixed economy (a blend of government regulation and free markets) are happily the wave of the future. I am, however, suggesting the church should have no part in talk that any capitalistic economy is the "best system possible."

Christians can never say "This is the best," because we profess that the kingdom of God is the best. Of course that kingdom will not be fully realized until time's end. But it is begun. And it is not our place to dictate how or where or when it may break in anew and more fully alleviate conditions of poverty or injustice. The deepest, most compelling aim for the church is not to support one economic system or another, but to measure the system one lives with against the claims of the kingdom, and attempt to live faithfully in the light of the consequent tension.

As I understand the perspective of the New Testament church, it is not consumed with either *tearing down* or *building up* a political or economic system. For the New Testament church such systems are simply givens. There is almost an indifference in Jesus' response to the questions about Caesar's coin, as if to say, "Give it to Caesar; it's got his picture on it." Likewise, Paul in Romans 13 merely assumes the existence of governmental authority. Go about your Christian business, he counsels; "be subject to the governing authorities" (v. 1). The government will approve when it considers your behavior good. Of course Paul, who was imprisoned by this very government and would die at its hands, knew it would not always recognize the true good. Certainly other New Testament writers realized the same—in Revelation 13, for instance, the Roman government is depicted as a horrible, damnable beast. When government does not recognize the true good, these writers were clear, you must follow God rather than Caesar.

Something like this is the real concern of passages like Romans 13:1-7 and 1 Peter 2:13-15, often used to counsel uncritical and full-scale support of the status quo. Such readings are often individualistic, forgetting that the New Testament presents the church as an alternative polity. In context, 1 Peter 2 urges the church itself to be a "holy nation," to witness as a social body against the surrounding darkness. So, too, must Romans 13 be read together with Romans 12. Then it is clear that the focus of the entire passage is not a philosophy of statecraft, but counsel on how the church can be the church—*its own unique political and social witness.* Romans 12 and 13:8-14 suggest how the gospel is lived in everyday, bodily situations (12:1-2): Submit to one another (12:3-8). Practice hospitality (12:9-13). Bless your enemies, live peaceably and forsake revenge (12:14-21). Care for your neighbor (13:8-10). Walk in the light of day which has come with the rising sun of the resurrection (13:11-14).

Thus, Romans 13:1-7 is erroneously lifted out of context when its words on government are made central to the meaning of Romans 12 and 13. Here, as in 1 Peter, the church is the central issue and government is peripheral. What matters *centrally* is not what the government does or fails to do. It is what the church does or fails to do in the steady, long haul of ordinary life, in the day-to-day nitty-gritty of human existence *under whatever governmental and economic system.*

All this, then, to say that the church's key responsibility is to live as the church, in the light of the kingdom, within a given host society. Christians are free to be grateful for the genuine blessings of capitalism. But we are also free—indeed, called—to see and respond to its flaws. We need to recognize how the success of capitalism is inimical to Christian family and the church's mission.

Yahweh as a Household God

Through most of history, the family was not separated from the wider world. As scholars Steven Mintz and Susan Kellogg write, a "sharp division between economics, religion, law, and politics and family was unimaginable." Before the Industrial Revolution, spouses, children, relatives and servants worked together in the household to produce goods. Economically, the household was a producing unit as well as a consuming unit. Only with nineteenth-century industrialization was the household privatized. Industrialization and the spread of factories introduced the single wage-earner, who departed the home to earn the family's livelihood. The household was no longer a center of economic productivity, where the family together wove rugs or cobbled shoes or farmed. (On farms, for instance, even young children could tend sheep or gather kindling.)

In the industrialized world the family also lost several of its other responsibilities. Gradually it would care less and less for its aged, provide little relief for its poor and little substantial education for its young. The panoply of services once issuing from the family were turned over to government, banks, insurance companies and schools.

In short, the family became a pale shadow of itself. It struggled for redefinition, for new purpose and meaning. And so the household was reconceived as a soft, inviting retreat from the hard, bruising world of commerce. The nonproductive household needed a wage-earner to venture into the bitter outside world. This was, of course, the husband and father, whose very soul and humanity were considered at danger as he was thrust into the marketplace.

A hit book of 1839, in both England and America, was Sarah Stickney Ellis's *The Women of England: Their Social Duties and Domestic Habits.* Ellis depicted her culture's novel, sharp division of the sexes and of the public and private worlds. Even as a boy, she wrote, the male learns to invest with "supreme importance, all considerations relating to the acquisition of wealth." But the boy also learned early that acquiring wealth meant plunging into a Hobbesian jungle of competition. For the man,

> there is no union in the great field of action in which he is engaged, but envy, and hatred, and opposition, to the close of the day—every man's hand against his brother, and each struggling to exalt himself, not merely by trampling upon his fallen foe, but by usurping the place of his weaker brother, who faints by his side, from not having brought an equal portion of strength into the conflict, and who is consequently borne down by numbers, hurried over and forgotten.

But if this is the lot of man, to be cast daily into the jungle, how does he avoid turning into a beast? He avoids it by returning each evening to a refuge of purity, cleansing and refreshment. It is a fact, Ellis claimed, "that gentlemen may employ their hours of business in almost any degrading occupation, and, if they have but the means of supporting a respectable establishment at home, may remain gentlemen still."

The task of the conscientious woman, then, was to stay safe and pure at home. Only so could she become for her husband (Ellis again) "a kind of second conscience, for mental reference, and spiritual counsel, in moments of trial." Ellis was quite explicit that faith belonged at home with women and children; she wrote of the home as a place where the man could "keep as it were a separate soul for his family, his social duty, and his God."

Ellis was not alone in such sentiments. Horace Bushnell called for good wives to keep a home filled with peace and the "pure atmosphere of silence." To this their husbands, "the poor bruised fighters," could return "to be quieted, and civilized, and get some touch of the angelic." John Ruskin urged woman to turn the family home into a "sacred place, a vestal temple, a temple of the hearth watched over by household gods," once more a refuge for the often wounded and "*always* hardened husband," the warrior in the field of commerce.

So the woman's main service to society was mostly indirect. She supported her husband's corrupting and wearisome forays into the public arena. But there was one societal service family and the domesticated woman could still perform directly. They could support a growing economy by *consuming* lavishly. So in this period was born the myth of the woman as natural shopper. The nineteenth-century philosopher Schopenhauer opined, "In their hearts, women think that it is men's business to earn money and theirs to spend it." Wags of the day suggested that Eve found her own leaf and inaugurated dressmaking, so women had an acquisitive nature from the start. Eduard von Hartmann, in his 1895 book *The Sexes Compared,* quite seriously complained that woman is prone to depression and even madness if she cannot shop as a diversion.

Now it certainly won't do to pretend the Industrial Revolution was all bad for the family. It has left us with many goods, including an astonishingly lower rate of infant mortality. But, again, we must recognize the ill as well as the good bequeathed us. With the rise of industrialization came the separation of life into compartments of public and private. Even today we are prone to think and imagine according to these divisions. The public world is male, productive and areligious.

The private world is female, consumption-oriented and religious.

For now, notice one remarkable problem with this arrangement: Christians have been oddly complicit in relegating God to only one part of life, the domestic. In effect (as Ruskin apparently noticed) we have reduced Israel's Creator Lord, the King of the universe, to the status of a household god. As historian Donald Meyer notes, religion became synonymous with family life, and *only* with family life. "It was hard to see how one could safely leave home at all. This was unsatisfactory. It would do no good for the family to conserve an ethic so exquisite it unfitted its members for society."

The Belligerence of the Bottom Line

With this bit of history we can see how capitalism as we know it has decentered the family and faith, pushing both to the periphery of the "real world." But we need to take a step further to appreciate the full economic challenge faced by the Christian family today.

Shortly after World War II, a retailing analyst named Victor Lebow spoke all too prophetically. "Our enormously productive economy," he said, "demands that we make *consumption our way of life, that we convert the buying and use of goods into rituals, that we seek our spiritual satisfaction,* our ego satisfaction, in consumption." What Lebow hoped for has come to pass, in fact succeeded all too well. Advanced capitalism has given us a world in which consumption is a way of life and even a religious act. Simply put, Western capitalism inhibits the Christian practice of family because the market has overrun its boundaries. We have come to see and conduct not just the bartering of bread and soap but the whole of our lives in the ways of the market. As Robert Bellah and his colleagues write, "The rules of the competitive market, not the practices of the town meeting or the fellowship of the church, are the real arbiters of living."

Consider the church itself. We are counseled, through books like *Marketing Your Ministry,* to reconceive the church's mission in terms of the professional marketers. We find newspaper reports such as this one, about a northern California church:

The members of St. John's Lutheran Church have a money-back guarantee. They can donate to the church for 90 days, then if they think they made a mistake, or did not receive a blessing, they can have their money back. The program is called "God's Guarantee" and the pastor is confident it will work. "We trust God to keep his promises so much that we are offering this money back policy," he said.

Or think of the practice of medicine, another realm once sacrosanct and kept carefully separate from the market. As I learned while my father slowly died of cancer some years ago, the market and economic calculus tend to engulf medicine's central aim of caring for the sick. Patients lie ill or dying in huge, bureaucratic hospitals—hospitals that must be huge and bureaucratic to afford capitalized, technologized medicine. Patients face intimidating, incredibly complex machinery. They are impersonally poked and probed by specialists who seem little more than technicians of the human body, and visited at most four or five minutes a day by a personal doctor. The number of days spent in a hospital is now blatantly determined on the basis of money, according to the limits of insurance coverage. Outpatient clinics and emergency services advertise and otherwise compete in the marketplace. As philosopher Jeffrey Stout writes, medicine truly "tends increasingly to be dominated by modes of interaction and patterns of thought characteristic of the market and the bureaucracies, where goods external to medical care reign."

I will cite one other example among many possibilities. Money and the economic calculus have also crossed the line into what we have called our private lives, and there also have become the measure of quality and worth. This was driven home to me when I recently read a magazine interview about friendship. The panel members were asked to explain what is good about friendship, but were stymied because they could attempt to understand friendship only in terms of the manager who keeps a constant eye on the market's bottom line. They said "time demands" weigh on couples seeking friends. Friendships were said to have "agendas"; they are "maintained" until they no longer serve a purpose, then are "terminated." Visits with friends are a matter of "organization" and "arrangement." An advantage of friendship is that it provides "accountability." And friendships must be viewed from the vantage point of "productivity," so that you "invest" in a friendship despite a society that fails to "promote" friendship.

What occurred to me after I read the article was that I've often heard family spoken of in the same distorting terms. Children present "time demands." Spouses should "invest" in one another to "promote" intimacy, or they may come to consider their marriage "unproductive." In this and many other ways, friendship and the family suffer from the belligerence of the bottom line. Once more, I don't mean by this that the market and profit motive are somehow evil in themselves, but that the market and profit motive have overrun their proper boundaries and invaded every aspect of our lives.

Indeed, Milton Friedman and his compatriots in what has come to be known as the Chicago school of economics now straightforwardly insist that we should let the market serve as the moral code defining all our lives. These economists tell us marriage is not so much about love as about supply and demand for spouses, that a man commits suicide when "the total discounted lifetime utility remaining to him reaches zero," and that we should take care of the shortage of infants for adoption by quoting baby prices like soybean futures.

Ironically, an earlier era's harried men and women imagined the tyranny of the bottom line could be escaped, if only in the bosom of the family. Now, it seems, there is nowhere to flee. In our postmodern world, the bottom line intrudes into and attempts to rule over all of life.

When Heaven Is a Supermarket

We could call this vision of life and morality the economic exchange model. Under the economic exchange model, persons are seen first and foremost as consumers. Consumers are autonomous, isolated and self-interested. They must be free to pursue whatever goods (or products) they desire. In fact, this is how goods are defined: goods are merely whatever people want. There is no common good, a good all should pursue together, nor is there any need to try to determine a common good. Instead, we need only allow individuals to associate—to work, play or live together—when such an association will serve each individual's self-interest. It is fine and right that an individual will associate with another individual only as long as self-interest is served. Relationships are contractual. They are binding only so long as (explicit or implicit) terms of the contract are fulfilled. When they are not, the contract is dissolved and the relationship "terminated."

Clearly this is an understanding of relationships as economic exchange. I will be your friend or your spouse—or attend your church—because you amuse me or enhance my mental health. But if you fail to "meet my needs" (say you bore me or reveal things about yourself that disturb me), I am probably wisest to seek another friend or spouse. Under the economic exchange model only I know what I want, which is to say only I know what is really good for me. There is no higher or overriding good to refer to, such as a good defined by a tradition or institution. (God, as in St. John's Lutheran Church and its money-back guarantee, is only the guarantor of what I have already determined is good.) So if we find ourselves wanting conflicting goods from one another, we may try to "negotiate" our differences and arrive at a compromise at least partly satisfactory to each of our self-interests. Or we may simply part amicably, returning separately to the free and wide marketplace of potential friends and spouses.

It bears repeating: in the economic exchange model, persons are first and foremost consumers. Consuming is the moral activity par excellence. We are by definition isolated and autonomous individuals, called to realize ourselves by the choices we must be free to make. This means our ideal world is one with as many choices as possible, about everything possible. So in 1976 the average American supermarket carried nine thousand products; today it stocks thirty thousand. The typical produce section in 1975 had 65 items; today it has 285. The median household, with cable, now picks up more than thirty TV stations. During the 1980s, a new periodical was born for every day of every year.

And in more serious matters, such as faith? My suburban telephone directory lists 137 churches, including not only eight varieties of Baptists but also the Nichiren Shoshu Temple (Buddhist), the Ahmadiyya Movement (Islam) and the Bochasanwasi Swaminarayan Sanstha (unidentified). Scholar Robert Webber has identified fourteen varieties of evangelicals, with variations within each variety. And in at least one area—Bible production—evangelicals sprint far ahead of the rest of the postmodern pack. At a rate pushing ten to twenty every year, our publishers release new Bibles customized for everyone from Vietnam veterans to collectors of the Precious Moments figurines.

In the postmodern world, heaven is a vast supermarket; hell is a corner drugstore stocking only one brand of aspirin or toilet paper—or more significantly, only one brand of religion or morality or marriage. And if life is a supermarket, I should live as if I have no history, no persisting identity that might bind me to a particular commitment and so at a later point rule out the pursuit of a new want or need. After all,

around the corner and in the next aisle may await some new and
improved product, beckoning me to switch brands.

Family in the Image of the Market

What would family look like under the economic exchange model?
Fortunately, there are still enough vestiges of other family models to
prevent the total domination of the economic exchange model. The
bourgeois model of family, for instance, is antagonistic to the economic
exchange model's diminished respect for the value of commitment. But
bourgeois family grew up hand in hand with capitalism, and so backers
of the bourgeois family (like James Robison and Jack Kemp) have been
reluctant to criticize capitalism's ill effects. They have not helped us
notice and feel our culture's tremendous pressures to create an economic exchange family. Thus we do see families that represent the
economic exchange model in part, and if we are honest, we probably
find ourselves thinking or acting in its terms all too often.

Family wrought in the image of the market puts a premium on
novelty rather than fidelity. People marry because the marriage will
serve their interests *as they understand them at the moment.* There is no
predicting how I may grow and change, or how my mate may. Commitment can therefore only be tenuous and heavily qualified. Like any
careful contract, our marriage should continually be open to reevalu-
ation. If at any point it fails to promote the self-actualization of one or
another spouse, we must have available the option of ending the partnership.

Consequently, under the economic exchange model, serial polygamy
(several mates serially, over a lifetime rather than all at once) is a
perfectly sensible practice. It is immoral to fail to become all I can
become as a person. And the ideal person is independent, aloof enough
to ever enter into new relationships (and end others), focused always

on the pursuit of self-interest. So in fact I have a *moral obligation* to divorce and seek a new mate if my original wife can no longer promote my growth and self-actualization.

Of course children may complicate divorces. But under the economic exchange model it is difficult to say why we should have children in the first place. Remember that in this model of life the ethic is above all one of individualism and autonomy, of keeping my choices open. This makes it irrational to bear a child, since children represent a commitment of several years. A child will limit my mobility, dictate the spending of much of my money and create "agendas" I would otherwise never have imagined for myself. (Which should accordingly make me especially averse to "unplanned" or handicapped children, who will even more radically affect my autonomy.) According to this model, it may even be immoral to have a child. Moral behavior, after all, is behavior that advances my interests, aids my self-realization. But if that is why I choose to have a child, I am using another person without consulting his or her wishes. By the very act of conceiving a child I am violating my child's autonomy, his or her highest good.

So swayed by the economic exchange model, we are indeed confused about why we have children and even if we should have children. Only under this model's dominance could we soberly create daycare centers that label children Precious Commodities, fixate on the monetary costs of rearing a child from diapers through college or seriously wonder whether we should "force" our faith and morality on our children.

But even redefined, family holds an uncertain place in a world formed after the image of the marketplace. As we have noted, the modern economy radically separated our public and private lives. Far from imagining family to have any sort of social or political task, we want under the economic exchange model to guard and protect it from the social and political. Yet in the process family has been trivialized and emptied of meaning. The home once served major economic and social functions. Now it is a "haven" from the "real world." It is a retreat for the wage-earner and a nest for children who await true personhood in the form of maturity and independence. All it can provide is affection and intimacy, which tend to be cheapened and diluted because they are not seen to have a tie to the truly significant wider world. This is affection and intimacy that are powerless to affect reality, affection and intimacy that quickly erode into mere "warm fuzzies."

One of the most insidious effects of the economic exchange model across our society is just this trivialization of what should be our noblest aims, attitudes and emotions. Trained as consummate consumers, we learn to adopt even religious faiths tentatively, with an eye to new options that may appear around the bend. No wonder we find it less and less credible to think anything might be worth dying for. But if nothing is worth dying for, is anything worth living for? Devoid of substantive purpose, our lives too easily degenerate into bland avoidance of pain and the unending search for new amusements. Shopping is the highest or essential form of life, as ironically recognized in the T-shirt adaptation of Descartes's axiom, "I shop, therefore I am." Our prophets are sucked into the marketing machinery and made one more "fad" or temporarily stimulating "movement." And even the most monumental events, such as the fall of the Berlin Wall, quickly become grist for soda-pop commercials. Of course, the fall of the Wall itself demonstrated that the dominance of the economic exchange model is not limited to North America. During the first days that East Germans were allowed to cross at will into West Germany, a graffiti sage scrawled on the Wall, "They came, they saw, they did a little shopping."

This, not the feminist movement, is the prime reason so many women find it demeaning and uninspiring to stay at home. Shopping really is not a very profound or exciting reason for living. The household removed from the public world is trivial and thin. And this is why adolescent children, who of course know their parents only at home—in what they are trained to view as an escape from the real world—see their parents as irrelevant and backward, and their growing-up years within the family as a sort of limbo, at best a playground without responsibilities, at worst a holding pen this side of reality.

Sharply privatizing family is the first step toward killing it. It is the unwitting placement, as it were, of the family on the gallows—even though the hanging rope has not been lowered and the trap door remains shut for the moment. Family needs purpose beyond itself and its sentimentality to survive and prosper. As Robert Nisbet writes,

> To suppose that the present family, or any other group, can perpetually vitalize itself through some indwelling affectional tie, in the absence of concrete, perceived functions, is like supposing that the comradely ties of mutual aid which have grown up incidentally in a military unit will outlast a condition in which war is plainly and irrevocably banished. . . .
>
> The family is a major problem in our culture simply because we are attempting to make it perform psychological and symbolic functions with a structure that has become fragile and an institutional importance that is almost totally unrelated to the economic and political realities of our society.

In short, family has been stripped of its wider and public significance and left only with intimacy and "private" relationships as its purpose. This has occurred at the same time the private was separated from the public and trivialized. Perhaps not so coincidentally, Christian faith was also removed from the public realm and trivialized. The great God Yahweh was tamed, domesticated, housebroken. Religion was made a private, individual and purely spiritual matter. Right and wrong in the marketplace and the public square—the "real world"—was no longer to be decided with any reference to the story of Israel and Jesus Christ. And finally economic calculus has invaded even the limited private world left to religion. Friendship and family itself are now increasingly regulated and controlled via the terms of the market.

Two Visions

Our crucial problem, then, is that the market has overrun its boundaries. The economic exchange model has become our dominating, even our religious, vision of life. The vision is religious in that it defines our reason for being, provides a purpose for living, gives us criteria by which to decide if we are failing or succeeding as persons. As novelist Don DeLillo writes, it has created a culture in which managers are the paramount heroes and financiers are more spiritual than monks. And it has given us a rule of relationships that says simply, "Whatever feels right, as long as you both want to do it and nobody gets hurt, there's no reason not to do it." Under such a rule, marriage is indeed a lost art.

But of course if this vision is religious, it is a direct challenge to the Christian vision. Our task then is to correct our vision. We must realize and learn to recognize our false vision, a vision that domesticates God, suspects fidelity, sees little place for children and trivializes the adventure of family. And we must return to our own story, the story of Israel and Jesus, and understand what family is for and about on those terms.

CHAPTER FOUR

CHURCH AS FIRST FAMILY

•

"He corrupts the young people. It all sounds fine: Blessed
are you who weep, for you will laugh. But what does he actually do? He makes parents weep over lost sons. He promises everything will change. But what actually changes?
Families are destroyed because children run away from
their parents."
A forlorn mother in Gerd Theissen's
fictional reconstruction of Jesus' career,
The Shadow of the Galilean

In the postmodern world the market and its ways have swallowed our
lives whole, so that living in genuinely Christian family is almost a lost
art. Recovering the purpose of Christian family, on the distinctive terms
of the Christian story, requires two declarations—one negative and one
positive.

The negative declaration: The family is not God's most important
institution on earth. The family is not the social agent that most significantly shapes and forms the character of Christians. The family is not
the primary vehicle of God's grace and salvation for a waiting, desperate world.

And the positive declaration: The church is God's most important

institution on earth. The church is the social agent that most significantly shapes and forms the character of Christians. And the church is
the primary vehicle of God's grace and salvation for a waiting, desperate world.

Putting the church first, of course, runs counter to the interpretation
of many evangelical traditionalists. They put biological family first.
They emphatically place family at the center of God's purposes and
work on behalf of the world. Traditionalist R. J. Rushdoony offers a
typical affirmation while commenting on Genesis 1:28, the mandate for
humanity to exercise dominion over all creation. This dominion, Rushdoony writes, "is essential to the life of church, state, and school, to arts
and sciences, to every calling and every phase of life, but, *in its primary
assignment and orientation, is given to the family. The central area of
dominion is . . . the family under God."*

Yet we cannot put Jesus first and still put family first. For Christians,
the primary creation account is not Genesis, but the first chapter of the
Gospel of John. There Genesis's opening words are directly quoted only
to be modified in the light of Christ: "In the beginning was the Word . . ."
(Jn 1:1). There we learn that "all things came into being" through the
Word and that "the Word became flesh and lived among us," bearing
the name Jesus (Jn 1:3, 14).

Of course, this hardly means we ignore Genesis and the rest of the
Old Testament. What we call the Old Testament was, after all, Jesus'
entire Bible, from which he learned and taught of God's grace and
power. But Jesus Christ is the lens through which Christians read the
Old and New Testaments (and through which we "read" the world as
well). In Calvin's language, Jesus is the prophet, priest and king who
recapitulates and crystallizes the story of Israel. Consequently we
should look back, all the way to creation, *through Jesus Christ.*

And our understanding of the family shifts if we read Scripture by beginning with Jesus. If Jesus comes before Genesis, then we must read the Genesis account of family's creation in the light of commands such as "Whoever comes to me and does not hate father and mother, wife and children, brothers and sisters, yes, and even life itself, cannot be my disciple" (Lk 14:26). And we must look anew at the covenant, a promise that certainly had a great deal to do with biological family.

The Centrality of Covenant

Each night, when Sandy and I put our daughter Jesselyn to bed, we play a tape of children's songs. Jesselyn especially enjoys the albums of the folksinger Raffi. And among her favorite Raffi songs is "All I Really Need," which affirms that the only things truly necessary to the good life are a song in your heart, a full belly and a loving family.

The ancient Hebrews would have agreed with Raffi and Jesselyn. For them, the richest blessings God offered came through family. Life was whole—a man or woman was whole—through marriage and the bearing of children. In fact, there was no Hebrew word for "bachelor"; the eunuch was impure; and the barren woman could hardly imagine a reason to go on living (see 1 Sam 1:3-8).

New Testament scholar William Countryman suggests that in Jesus' day the centrality of the family must have been "as close to a self-evident truth" as any in Israel. Rabbis placed limits on how long a man might abstain from intercourse with his wife. Not bearing children was equal to shedding blood and diminishing the image of God. Procreation was an obligation; sometimes a minimum number of children was specified. A Rabbi Abba declared that one question sure to be asked at the judgment would be "Did you engage in procreation?"

Of course, Israel had profound reasons for such a profound valuing of family. With a promise, a covenant call, the great father Abraham was pulled from his homeland of Ur of the Chaldees. The promise drawing him away was the assurance that if he went, "I [God] will make of you a great nation, and I will bless you" (Gen 12:2). Abraham's family would grow into families and, finally, a nation, and through it "all the families of the earth [would] be blessed" (Gen 12:3). God repeatedly reminded Abraham of this promise: his descendants would number as the stars, or as the grains of sand on a seashore (Gen 15:5; 22:7).

So God would bless the entire world through the children, the lineage, of this specific people Israel. The significance and excitement of family were only heightened when a messiah in the line of David was anticipated: a certain man and woman would actually bear the great one who would fulfill Israel's world-shaping destiny.

This put marriage and family at the marrow of Israel's identity and purpose. They were the greatest signs of Israel's election by God. The prophets could use marriage as a metaphor of the ups and downs of the relationship between God and Israel (Is 50:1; 54:6; Jer 3:1, 7-8, 20; Ezek 16:23; Hos 2:19-20). And, of course, the God whom Israel came to know through that God's free, grace-full promise making and promise keeping (the covenant) is the Creator-God. This God is the one who calls humankind into families, to "be fruitful and multiply, and fill the earth and subdue it" (Gen 1:28). Thus Karl Barth nicely summarizes the Old Testament estimate of marriage: "Not only in marriage, to be sure, but primarily and supremely in marriage, God manifests Himself in His unity as Creator-God and God of the covenant, who as such is the God of free, electing grace."

Can Bachelors Keep the Covenant?

But wait. The one Christians consider the Davidic Messiah has come. And by these Hebrew definitions Jesus who is worshiped as the Christ was not blessed. He took no wife; he bore no children. He called some to be "eunuchs." One of his greatest followers, the apostle Paul, could declare it better to remain single than to marry (1 Cor 7). Jesus and the early church did not wholly embrace the family, which until then had been the indispensable vehicle of the covenant. Were they, then, rejecting the covenant? How could the covenant possibly be kept apart from blood and kin?

Biblical scholarship widely affirms that those who followed Moses out of Egypt were a ragtag collection of slaves—even of different races and places of origin. As Exodus 12:38 notes, a "mixed multitude" left Egypt (RSV). In a real sense, the exodus created the people Israel. It was not bloodstream, racial stock or language that set early Israel apart from its neighbors. It was a particular tradition, the living and developing tradition of a people that responded to a promise-making God who acted decisively in Egypt—and who was then seen, through that lens, to have acted earlier in *parts* of what had become the people Israel. (The most significant parts were, of course, the lines of Abraham, Isaac and Jacob.) As Old Testament scholar John Bright writes, "Speaking theologically, one might with justice call Israel a family; but from a historical point of view neither her first appearance nor her continued existence can be accounted for in terms of blood kinship."

A rough comparison to the history of the United States might clarify. Exactly when did America begin? The answer is not simple. There were native American Indians here centuries before Columbus sailed in 1492. Then came the Pilgrims in the seventeenth century. The Revolutionary War and break from England occurred in the late eighteenth century. But even then it could be said that the United States of America *as a single, unified people* did not yet exist. As historians emphasize, before the Civil War the United States of America *were—they* remained separate and plural. After the Civil War the United States of America *is*—the states are one and, defying proper grammar, singular. It was the event of the Civil War, with the victory of those favoring union, that consolidated and made whole a vast territory and different peoples.

So, without error or contradiction, we can say the United States of America began thousands of years ago, with the native Indians who fished its streams and hunted its forests "before the Romans thought of Rome" (to quote singer Bruce Cockburn). We can say it began in 1492, with the arrival of a fortune-seeking Spaniard. Or we can start with the story of the English colonists, in the 1600s. Yet again, we can justifiably put the United States's inception at 1776, with the Declaration of Independence. And finally, we can argue indisputably that the collection of states really became a nation in 1865, at the end of the Civil War.

Similarly, we need not at all deny the importance of Abraham, Isaac and Jacob to recognize that Israel became a solid, unified people only with the exodus and the covenants that followed it. The comparison of Abraham Lincoln to Moses, which emancipated slaves were so apt to make, works on more than one level. Both Lincoln and Moses worked with preexisting but loosely confederated peoples; both, in a sense, were founders of a single nation.

So John Bright's point is important. At the root of the covenant people, and so of the covenant itself, is not mere blood and kin. Certainly early Israel had some ties of biological family. But it was more crucially and comprehensively drawn together theologically, by the acts of God in history.

And if the covenant was *made* apart from blood and kin, it could be *kept* apart from blood and kin. In our parlance, as in that of the ancient Greeks, *son* or *daughter* primarily entails biological descent. But in Hebrew thought, to be a son or daughter was not primarily a matter of biological descent. Instead, it was primarily a matter of obedience. Israel's election as the "children of God" entailed obedience (Deut 13:17—14:2). If Israel disobeyed, God might spurn "his sons and daughters" (Deut 32:19-20), sell them into slavery (Is 50:1) and declare them no longer God's people (Hos 1:9).

This strain of thought shines clear in the New Testament. In the parable of the prodigal son, the disobedient prodigal confesses to his father, "I am no longer worthy to be called your son" (Lk 15:11-32). The writer of Hebrews suggests that if disciples are not disciplined (that is, made obedient) by God, "then you are illegitimate and not his children" (Heb 12:8).

It was most likely in this spirit—a covenant spirit—that Jesus turned away his biological mother and brothers and declared instead, "Whoever does the will of God is my brother and sister and mother" (Mk 3:31-35). Jesus' primary family is not composed of those who share his genetic makeup, but of those who share his obedient spirit.

There can be no doubt that Jesus displaced the biological family. For those who would follow him, family could no longer be paramount in the service of God. And there can be no doubt that this displacement shocked and dismayed many—perhaps most—of those who heard his words and saw his deeds. But Jesus did not act without precedent or resource in the covenant that was Israel's foundation and core. Instead, he implicitly emphasized the essence of covenant itself. Covenant is a promise. And promises are not brute facts of nature. They are made, and accepted or rejected, in the turbulent flow of history. At one with the prophets and the Deuteronomic tradition, Jesus indicated, "The living God, whom we have learned to be the creator of heaven and earth, this God has made a promise. By this promise you may become his sons and daughters. If you embrace the promise and live by it, you are God's children. If you turn your back on the promise, you denounce your rightful parenthood and destiny. Which will it be?"

How the Kingdom Threatened the Family

I have just used the language of covenant, or promise, to encapsulate

Jesus' message. At the beginning of his Gospel, Mark reports Jesus' words to be, more exactly, "The time is fulfilled, and the kingdom of God has come near; repent, and believe in the good news" (1:15).

It was the centrality and immediacy of the kingdom that made Jesus' life and message so shocking. In our time, it is difficult to appreciate the impact of Jesus' kingdom proclamation and work. This may especially be the case in evangelical circles, where the kingdom has often been privatized and spiritualized. Frequently the kingdom is understood to be something that comes only in the individual's heart, through a one-on-One relationship with God. And salvation's fullness is anticipated to come after death, in heaven, quite apart from any life on earth. Such a kingdom is so private, ethereal and future that it can have little to do with a social, bodily and present institution such as the family.

But all this is a serious distortion of what the kingdom means in the New Testament (and so a distortion of Christian family as well). Crucially, Jesus lived and died as a Palestinian Jew. In his world and thought, God was expected to act for the liberation and restoration of Israel, the covenant nation. This is why, for instance, Jesus gathered a new community of twelve disciples: they were symbolic of the twelve tribes of Israel. The broad Hebrew and Jewish expectation was a salvation not merely for individual souls, but for nations and the earth itself. Thus Isaiah foresaw a day when God would bless archenemy Egypt as his people and another archenemy, Assyria, as "the work of my hands" (Is 19:25), and a day when wolf would live with lamb (Is 11:6). None of this is forgotten in the New Testament, where God's redemption includes the groaning creation (Rom 8) and will consummate in a new heaven *and a new earth* (Rev 21:1).

So Jesus does not merely call individuals *qua* individuals, who will separately and simply await death and the bodiless joys of heaven. Instead, he forms a community on earth. He declares that the new age

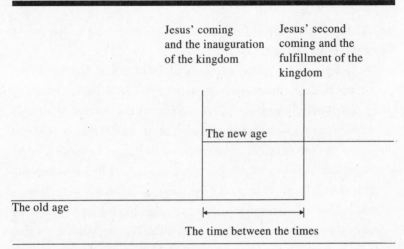

Figure 2.   The Time Between theTimes

of the kingdom has arrived and shows that it has physical implications (he heals and feeds) and social implications (forgiveness reconciles and so restores community; acceptance of the outcasts and defense of the poor challenge injustice).

Certainly the old age and its ways continue. The Romans do not fall down and worship the God of Israel. The rich and powerful of the world do not stop oppressing the poor and powerless of the world. Even now, we still await the total eclipse of the old age by the new age begun in Jesus.

Nonetheless, Jesus spoke in the present tense: "The time *is* fulfilled." And Paul later affirmed that in Jesus "the fullness of time had come" (Gal 4:4). So despite the lingering of the old age, the new age has begun. And Jesus' community is called to recognize the new age and live in its light. Here is a community that among the world's fractured and divided communities will live in unity and truth, worshiping the God of Israel, who is Lord of all creation. That is why Jesus' ethic is a social ethic—a way of life not for isolated individuals but for individuals in community. In fact, it is a way of life for new individuals in a new family. As biblical scholar Gerhard Lohfink writes,

> The question whether the demands of Jesus can be fulfilled is not one which can ultimately be answered by an individual, especially an individual sitting at a desk. Jesus' ethic is not directed to isolated individuals, but to the circle of disciples, the new family of God, the people of God which is to be gathered. It has an eminently social dimension. Whether or not this ethic can be fulfilled is something that can only be determined by groups of people which consciously place themselves under the reign of God and wish to be real communities of brothers and sisters—communities which form a living arena for faith, in which everyone draws strength from each other.

Those who heard and saw Jesus the Nazarene were confused and perplexed, but they correctly understood that the kingdom he hailed had immediate social and "worldly" effects. In their understanding, the kingdom would change the dreams and attitudes—the "heart"—of individuals, and that was extremely important. But the kingdom's coming would change individual attitudes exactly because it would change the wider world. Thus Mary, celebrating the Messiah she will bear into the world, sings of political effects ("he has brought down the powerful from their thrones") and economic effects (he "has sent the rich away empty") (Lk 1:52-53). And because it would change and redescribe the entire world, the kingdom's coming would create new and terrible conflicts of allegiance: conflicts with the state, with religions, with neighbors—and even with the biological family.

First Family Is the Church

It is no accident that Gerhard Lohfink uses the language of kinship and describes the body of Christ as "the new family of God." With the coming of the kingdom—a kingdom that manifests itself physically as well as spiritually, socially as well as individually, and in the present as well as in the future—Jesus creates a new family. It is the new first family, a family of his followers that now demands primary allegiance. In fact, it demands allegiance even over the old first family, the biological family. Those who do the will of the Father (who, in other words, live under the reign of God) are now brothers and sisters of Jesus and one another. Jesus can speak even more challengingly: he forthrightly declares that the advent of the kingdom means brother will turn against brother, children against parents and parents against children (Mt 10:21-22). So far as the biological family is concerned, "I have not come to bring peace, but a sword" (Mt 10:34). Those who love father or mother more than Jesus, this Jesus says, are not worthy of him (Mt 10:37).

The consequences were real, visible and disturbing. In some cases parents and children really were turned against each other. One potential disciple was ready to come after Jesus, but asked first to bury his father (Lk 9:57-60). Jesus' rejoinder—"Let the dead bury their own dead"—was blunt and harsh. In the ancient world it was extremely important to see that one's parent received a proper burial. Among Jews, this was understood as nothing less than a requirement of the fourth commandment, to honor father and mother. In his setting, Jesus could hardly have more vividly or controversially asserted that allegiance to the kingdom of God precedes allegiance to the family.

This is exactly the way we should put it: Allegiance to the kingdom *precedes* the family. It does not destroy the family. Jesus affirmed the existence of the family in a number of ways.

He spoke strenuously against divorce (Mt 19:3-12). Asked by the Pharisees if a man might divorce his wife, Jesus grounded marriage in creation (saying that "the one who made them at the beginning 'made them male and female' "). Placing marriage in that context affirmed and even exalted it. It meant that a marriage is sacred, in the sense that its existence and rightness are beyond human manipulation. In Jesus' words, "What God has joined together, let no one separate."

Jesus also welcomed children and recognized the importance of their nurture, desiring to bless them (Mk 10:13-16; Lk 18:15-17). Children were among the marginal and easily neglected people of Jesus' day. He spoke against such neglect when he said, "Whoever welcomes one such child in my name welcomes me, and whoever welcomes me welcomes not me but the one who sent me" (Mk 9:37).

Finally, Jesus affirmed the family when he condemned those who defrauded their parents of wealth and due honor through the abusive use of the Corban (Mk 7:9-13). Corban was an oath dedicating funds to the use of the temple. Once property was so vowed, it could not be used for any other purpose, even helping destitute parents. Historical evidence indicates that some children used Corban to punish or wish evil on their parents, perhaps making the vow in the heat of anger. By condemning such use of the Corban, Jesus affirmed the fourth commandment. In fact, by not allowing even sacred vows to interfere with the duty to honor parents, he may actually have intensified the familial demands placed on the Jewish son or daughter.

So Jesus did not expect biological family to be denied or eliminated. He did, however, decenter and relativize it. He did not see it as the vehicle of salvation. He expected first family, the family of the kingdom, to grow evangelistically rather than biologically (Mt 28:19-20). Entrance to the kingdom in fact required a second birth, this time of water and the Spirit (Jn 3:5-6). Now for those who follow Jesus, the critical blood, the blood that most significantly determines their identity and character, is not the blood of the biological family. It is the blood of the Lamb.

Mary: Mother or Disciple First?

Compellingly, all this is true for Jesus' biological mother, Mary. Early
in two Gospels, angels greet her with the news that she will bear the
Messiah. She shares the joys of pregnancy with Elizabeth, the mother
of John the Baptist. When is a woman more excited about motherhood
than during the early months of pregnancy? Yet even here, amid all the
euphoria of approaching childbirth, Luke singles Mary out not as a
mother but as a disciple. She is a willing and obedient servant of God
who opens herself up simply and completely, saying, "Here am I, the
servant of the Lord; let it be with me according to your word" (Lk 1:38).
Thus a tension will be born with the child. Who is Mary, first and
foremost, in relation to Jesus: his mother or his disciple?

Luke will remember the child Jesus' leaving his parents without
notice and going to his "Father's house" to hear and question the
teachers (Lk 2:41-52). Mark will frankly recall that Mary at one point
feared her son mad and "went out to restrain him" (Mk 3:20-34). John
will have the young adult Jesus address his mother impersonally as
"woman" (Jn 2:4). We are not told much about Mary and her struggles,
but these are clear hints that she did struggle. At times she must have
felt her son disrespectful; she could think that he had lost his senses;
she obviously feared for his safety. She strained to understand who this
beloved but disconcerting flesh-of-her-flesh was and what he was
about.

The stakes were high. We should recall that Mary lived in a patriarchal society, a world in which a woman was thought to achieve her
highest calling, to discover her deepest self, through motherhood. So
Jesus' identity surely raised consuming questions about Mary's own
identity. Determining his identity would determine her identity. Again,
was she first of all his mother or his disciple?

And Jesus would not let Mary escape the dilemma of her true

identity. Consider more closely the episode Mark recounts in his third
chapter, when Jesus' family thinks he has lost his mind.

Mark's Gospel begins with a breathless tone of urgency. The Spirit
"immediately" drives Jesus into the wilderness (1:12); the fishermen
"immediately" leave their nets to follow Jesus (1:18); Jesus "immediately" calls James and John to himself (1:20); a sick woman is told about
this new healer "at once" (1:30); leprosy leaves a man "immediately"
(1:42), and Jesus sends him away "at once" (1:43). By the time Mark
barrels into his third chapter, Jesus has raised so much fuss that the
Pharisees have "immediately conspired" to destroy him (3:6).

Only now, in this tense, charged atmosphere—already caught up in
a dangerous momentum—will Mary make her initial appearance in
Mark's Gospel. The "multitudes" are clamoring after Jesus. The relig-
ious/political authorities are aroused. Jesus can only threaten them
further as he names twelve disciples—for his culture, a clear signal of
his messianic pretensions, that he plans to restore the twelve tribes of Israel
(3:13-19). Babbling gossip carries the message that Mary's son has gone
mad (3:21). The scribes suspect he is in league with Satan (3:22).

And Mary comes. She comes as mother. Her son stands in great peril.
So she brings his brothers to "restrain him," to protect him from himself
and his mission (3:21). Unable to reach her eldest son through the
crowd, the desperate mother sends word: "Your mother and your brothers and sisters are outside, asking for you" (3:32).

But the word that comes back to Mary is Jesus' refusal to see her.
Gesturing at the disciples around him, he says, "Here are my mother
and my brothers! Whoever does the will of God is my brother and sister
and mother" (3:34-35). If Mary and her other children cannot accept
Jesus' vocation, he cannot recognize their kindredness. Mary comes as
mother; her son calls her to something even more fundamental—he calls
her to discipleship.

Finally, John's Gospel sees the dying Jesus address Mary's dilemma of identity. As she stands beneath the cross with the disciple Jesus especially loved, Jesus says, "Woman, here is your son." And to the disciple he says, "Here is your mother" (Jn 19:25-27). At the foot of the cross—where, by Christian accounts, all true identities are revealed—Mary's dilemma is resolved. She is only secondarily the mother of Jesus. She is first of all his disciple. In her new first family, she has a new son, new sisters and brothers. In this family those who do the will of God are her closest relatives.

Paul's First Family

This sense of church as first family is striking in the letters of the apostle Paul. His high estimation of the church is obvious, and he uses a great deal of expressive imagery in an attempt to capture its importance and richness. But his most significant language for describing the church is the language of family. For Paul, Christians are children of God and brothers and sisters to one another (see, for instance, 1 Thess 1:4, 6). The phrase "my brothers" occurs more than sixty-five times in his letters. Paul can also call members of a church "my children" (as in 1 Cor 4:14 or Gal 4:19). Both the number and intensity of these familial phrases make Paul's letters remarkable in their time and place.

Our initial tendency may be to soften such language by imagining it as a sort of pious nicety. After all, many of us have been in churches where getting addressed as "Sister Elaine" or "Brother Tom" meant little more than a store clerk's polite salutation of a customer as "Ma'am" or "Sir." But Paul's use of kinship language is much more serious.

On a practical and even mundane level, it is significant that the church Paul knew met in households. Here were not gathered the two hundred or one thousand or two thousand people who meet weekly in our contemporary churches. A house in Paul's world could hold thirty people, forty-five or fifty at most, and therefore Pauline churches were small and intimate. Paul expected and depended on Christians' opening their homes (and thus their biological families) to Christian brothers and sisters (Rom 16:5; 1 Cor 16:15; Col 4:15; Philem 2). Such hospitality extended to a wide network of Christians, including missionaries and those on business trips (2 Cor 8:23). By so opening their homes, these Christians in effect recognized and welcomed "relatives" near and distant.

For Paul, then, it is no accident that the church's central sacrament, the Eucharist or Lord's Supper, recalls a daily domestic activity. The biological family recognizes the joyful need to feed its own and solidify its union with common meals; the church does the same when it gathers for the Eucharist (1 Cor 11:17-34).

On a more basic level, Paul crucially links familial language with baptism. The Gospel of John recognizes a need for the disciple of Jesus to be "born again," to know a second birth that redefines identity and admits the disciple to a family-community that will nurture the new identity. Paul has similar concerns but addresses them with the language of adoption rather than birth (Rom 8:15-17; Gal 3:26–4:6). He reminds believers that they have a new identity because they have been baptized into Christ. When children are adopted they take on new parents, new sisters and brothers, new names, new inheritances. And those who have been baptized into Christ, according to Paul, have been adopted by God. This baptism means Christians' new parent is God the Father ("Abba!" cries Paul). Their new siblings are other Christians. Their new name or most fundamental identity is simply "Christian"—one of those who know Jesus as Lord and determiner of their existence. And their new inheritance is freedom, community and resources provided a hundredfold (Mk 10:28-31).

Thus Paul's talk of adoption means that conversion is profound and thoroughgoing. Conversion creates a new person—even a new world (2 Cor 5:17). It involves nothing short of resocialization. The biological family, though not at all despised or useless, is no longer the primary source of identity, support and growth. As biblical scholar Wayne Meeks writes, "The natural kinship structure into which the person has been born and [which] previously defined his place and connection with society is here supplanted by a new set of relationships."

If we are still tempted to think of Paul's address of "brother" or "sister" as merely salutary, we should recall that such talk—and what lay behind it—was a key reason the early church suffered persecution. This church considered itself the believer's first and most fundamental family. And through baptism, Eucharist, hospitality and mutual aid, it was *in practice* the believer's first and most fundamental family. Theologian Rowan Greer notes that "however sympathetic one may be to early Christianity, it is impossible to avoid the conclusion that persecution was a natural response to it and that the popular prejudice against Christians had a basis in fact. The Roman world rightly saw that one possible implication of Christianity was a rejection of the social order." This was this so, Greer continues, not least because "the rejection of the family that often characterized Christianity in the age of the martyrs often carried with it the notion of the Church as a new and true family."

New Testament scholar N. T. Wright affirms the centrality of what I am calling first family in even more dramatic terms. Noting that "from baptism onwards, one's basic family consisted of one's fellow-Christians," he writes:

The fact of widespread persecution, regarded by both pagans and Christians as the normal state of affairs within a century of the beginnings of Christianity, is powerful evidence of the sort of thing Christianity was, and was perceived to be. It was a new family, a third "race," neither Jew nor Gentile but "in Christ."

Finally, sociologist Robert Nisbet places yet more emphasis on the political tension created by the church's belief that it was first family. In Nisbet's view, the deepest conflict between the church and the empire was not at a political but at a familial level. Christianity's strategy from the beginning was "to denigrate so far as possible the historic and still deeply rooted kinship tie and to offer the community of Christ as itself the only real and true form of kinship." Nisbet's words could be more nuanced, but he is exactly right to conclude that so far as early believers were concerned, the church was "the highest of all types of family."

A Genuine Reconciliation

I hope by now the two-sided declaration at the beginning of this chapter makes sense. The story of Israel and Jesus helps us to see that the nuclear family is not God's most important earthly institution. It is not the social agent that most significantly shapes and forms the character of Christians.

Indeed, as we saw in earlier chapters, the family has taken many shapes and forms throughout history. There is nothing about family, simply as a collection of spouses and offspring, that makes its members Christian. Instead, families and individuals gain a distinctive Christian identity through their participation in the church and its story. In the church we are "born again" and resocialized as a peculiar people whose lives would make no sense if the God of Israel and Jesus Christ were not living and true.

And so within the church, Christian nuclear families can resist the social forces that would remake the family in the image of the economic exchange model. That, at least, will be the argument of the subsequent chapters of this book.

The important point is that the church and its story give us an alternative place to stand. The postmodern world makes no "official" pretense of being Christian. It is profoundly fragmented, a confusing world without a center. And though the market may be increasingly dominant, in some sense an organizing center, it does not create a religious or moral center. Instead, as the marketing mentality pervades religion and morality, we are confronted with a growing array of religions and moralities to "meet every need."

So outside the church, isolated from it, individual families are simply caught in competing cultural currents. On the wild whitewater of post-modernity, the church is a kind of ark—providing a place to stand, companionship with others of like mind and imagination, and a rudder to guide in a society that has otherwise lost direction.

On this ark, furthermore, individual Christians can sail with hope and some safety back into the troubled waters of their own biological families. For even though we have for nearly two centuries attempted to sentimentalize the family, it is still inevitably a dangerous place.

Because of the awesome power of family ties, sentimental family can destroy the very people it so wants to love. Family ties can be power-fully supporting, holding us up, drawing us to safety after a misstep. But the ties that bind us in unity can also bind us in captivity. They can be stifling, oppressive, destructive. Most of us, as adults, have had the experience of going "home" to our parents and finding ourselves subtly forced back into slots and categories we long ago outgrew. The serious, thoughtful person becomes once again the family clown. The responsi-ble, competent career woman regresses to the status of baby daughter and youngest sister. The family rebel, long since settled into neighbor-hood and steady job, finds himself fighting with siblings and parents.

The claims of biological family are constant and frequently over-weening. You are *supposed* to love your sister, defer to your father,

indulge your mother. We think it is a law of nature, whether or not you
or anyone in your family has chosen—consciously and as a mature
person—to love one another. Of course, this is in many ways a great
comfort. It is no small privilege to have a place where "when you go
there, they have to take you in." But if that givenness, that biological
necessity, is without qualification, then family can all too easily abso-
lutize itself. Family loyalty can become ultimate loyalty. Family can
become the place you have to go and have to be taken in even if you
don't want to be taken in, even if it means denying the self you have
discovered as your real self. Then family is fate rather than destiny.
Then family ties bind destructively rather than constructively.

The gospel calls family beyond its natural state. It asks if we can *own*
love for our parents and siblings. It severs the family ties so that we can
choose whether to remake them. Family ties in their "natural" or
biological sense are coercive—they expect and demand love. Yet of
course that is contradictory. Love cannot be coerced into existence.
Love is given freely, or it is not at all love that is given. The gospel and
the kingdom enable us to choose our biological family, to affirm the
love it has already created and nurtured, to freely accept the circle we
were born into. In the light of the kingdom, family is not just an alien
fate that befell us; it is a gift of God that we can now claim as our
destiny.

The kingdom and the reality of church as first family deny the right
of biological family to be the whole world for any of its members. For
of course any family that attempts to be the world for itself in fact
creates a stunted, shrunken world. Paradoxically, a family is enriched
when it is decentered, relativized, recognized as less than an absolute.

When family is not the whole world, parents can let children go and
in turn find themselves reclaimed as parents. Truly letting a child go is
hard, not only because of the pain of separation, but because a child

fully released will reclaim and reshape the relationship in a way that may not be entirely to the parents' liking. This will especially be the case where the wounds and bruises of childhood are deep. In those situations some parents will want to insist that the past is done and gone, to imagine a sentimental and idyllic childhood.

I have a friend who, as a child, was hit on the back with a belt, repeatedly slapped so hard his ears rang. My friend Patrick was severely abused; his scars are not just physical. But when Patrick was grown up, his father wanted him to forget the abuse, to remember only the happy times. In so doing he was blocking Patrick in the reclamation and redemption of the only childhood he has—the real one, every bit of it.

A sentimentalized family necessarily remains infantile and undeveloped. It retains its biological basis (that can never be erased), but it fails to build on that basis and develop toward a richer maturity. In such cases it is likely that parents never were comfortable with the extrabiological aspects of family. They probably always wanted their offspring to be more clones, mere reflections of themselves, than persons. It is sad but true that some Christians will never be able to change this expectation. If their parents refuse to let family grow and develop and be enlivened spiritually as well as biologically, mature Christians can do little other than respectfully withdraw. They may keep contact and express concern for the family, but they cannot buy into its illusions or feed the destructive lies it circulates. So within the false world of such a family, they are likely to be seen as traitors and outsiders. Jesus' words about coming with a sword to divide families will be painfully real to them.

On the other hand, there are those who refuse to be responsible by denying the biological family's natural claim on them. They are those who think they owe nothing to their parents and insist they are nothing like their siblings. They cannot stand the thought of being indebted, though they are in fact inescapably indebted. They are like the son in the 1988 film *Da,* who sends his Irish father support money and then, after his da's death, learns that the money was never spent and is now being returned to him through a will. Thinking of his father, the distraught son cries, "I'll never forgive you for this, never!" Since he was born, he says, his father gave him money for his needs and desires. "When did I ever get a chance to pay it back, to be out from under, to be quit of you?" It's clear he sent the money in an attempt to deny any present *or past* dependence on his father, to cancel all debt and "be quit" of biological family.

But honest maturity requires admitting and embracing our dependence, accepting a debt that can never be canceled. No money can repay what our parents have given us. We would not be who we are or where we are without our family. Our best and truest hope is not to advance to some place where we owe nothing to our family, to create ourselves apart from all that has been given. Instead, our best and truest hope is to be freed to claim and accept what was given, to build on the good and redeem what is redeemable of the bad. What the gospel enables and expects is, in Karl Barth's words, not the destruction but "the radical renewal of the child-parent relationship," not the "separation of these kinsfolk" but their "genuine reconciliation, not merely in the peace of this transient world, but in the prospect of the perfection of the kingdom."

CHAPTER FIVE

THE SUPERIORITY
OF SINGLENESS

•

The most reliable callings are born from reflecting
on a situation that is more or less imposed on us. A
vocation is nearly always a way of accepting a situation
that was first of all considered a limitation.

Roger Mehl, *Love and Society*

It may seem curious for a book about Christian family to devote an
entire chapter to singleness. Frankly, most churches treat their singles
ministries as little more than sanctified substitutes for singles bars.
They see singles as peripheral to the core or central members, who
belong to families. They assume that the "normal" single will sooner or
later marry and start a family. True to these assumptions, a church in
my area once called its adult social group "Pairs and Spares."

I want to turn these assumptions upside down. I want to take Jesus
and Paul at their word that singleness is, *in some ways,* a better way of
life for Christians than marriage (see Mt 19 and 1 Cor 7). In fact, a right
understanding and practice of singleness is crucial to the health of
Christian family—especially in a postmodern world. To put it strongly,
there is at least one sure sign of a flawed vision of the Christian family:
it denigrates and dishonors singleness.

Let me begin to explain with the story of my friend Damien. In many ways Damien is someone to envy. He is gifted athletically. His looks and charm mean that he has never had to struggle to find female companionship. He shines in music enough that three colleges offered him scholarships to study piano. But unlike many people with artistic talent, he has a fine analytic and scientific mind—his parents wanted him to go to medical school.

Damien is one of those rare people who really could "do anything." If his high-school classmates agreed on anything, we agreed on that. But despite all this, I do not envy Damien. Today he lives on the West Coast. He has a decent and respectable job as a postman, but it frustrates him. His work exercises few of his remarkable abilities.

And Damien is unsatisfied with the rest of his life. He is, in his words, "afraid" to marry, and continues to cycle through initially intense and finally catastrophic relationships with women. Adept at so many things, he has never settled on any one interest long enough to excel at it in our highly specialized society. His connections with churches, volunteer organizations and hobby groups have been erratic and short-lived.

When we talked awhile back, Damien was depressed. We reflected, once again, on an array of options: return to school, get counseling to work on relationships, take a postal service job in Alaska and so forth. But then Damien sighed and said, "You know, freedom can be a curse."

Damien is a true citizen of the postmodern world. As we have seen, our postmodern world is a world of many markets. It presents us with an astounding array of options—options about what we eat and wear, the kind of person we might marry, how long we will stay in a marriage or any other kind of relationship, what religion we might follow, the job we will work at, what politics we will support, the sort of psycho-therapy we will try, the car we will buy, and on and on.

And our postmodern culture leaves us free to choose, to daily make dozens of trivial and often monumental choices. Surely this freedom is one of our highest goods. I certainly am not eager to give it up. But, like Damien, I feel some ambivalence about it. Our culture gives us all sorts of options, a breadth of freedom never before enjoyed in human history, but it gives us no help at all in knowing what or how to choose.

We have, in fact, defined freedom in a solely negative fashion. As the philosopher Isaiah Berlin writes, "By being free . . . I mean not being interfered with by others. The wider the area of non-interference the wider my freedom." Freedom, in other words, is being left alone. So in practical terms, Damien and the rest of us postmoderns can quickly point to all kinds of things we are free *from,* but we have little to say about what we are free *for.* We have an abundance of freedom, but what are we supposed to do with it? Can we do anything with it besides continually exercise it negatively, by going from one car to another, one job to another, one church to another, one spouse to another?

Now more than ever, Christian singleness is key because *it uniquely witnesses to true Christian freedom.* Without the faithful living of Christian singles, married Christians and the rest of the world cannot know what it means to be genuinely, fully free. Of course, I do not have in mind the kind of freedom reflected in tired jokes about marriage as enslavement: the proverbial bachelor's liberty to carouse is one of the more trite examples of negative freedom. Instead, an understanding of the New Testament's appreciation of freedom and singleness holds many surprises, exactly because there are so many misconceptions about the Bible, sex and singleness.

I have said Jesus and Paul hold up singleness as, in certain ways, a better way of life for Christians than marriage. But how, exactly? In what ways? The church and Christian tradition have sometimes been repressive, even flatly wrong, about marriage, singleness and the whole issue of sexuality. We need to reexamine the reasons for seeing single-ness as good so that, in a confused and searching postmodern world, we can reassert the goodness of singleness for the right reasons. Only so, as we shall see, can we reassert the goodness of family, and the goodness of freedom, for the right reasons.

Augustine's Wrong Turn

Maybe we best begin by trying to get at the root of the church's confusion about sexuality. For most of its history, the church has considered sexual feelings and expression at least remotely sinful. Though ever so chastely, virginity and saintliness have gone hand in hand.

Perhaps to a man, the church fathers exalted virginity. Many would agree with the sentiment of Gregory of Nazianzus, who warned of the "soul's unlovely love for lovely bodies." Much of this had to do with the widespread cultural attitudes of the world inhabited by early Christianity. If early Christians were what we would call prudes, they weren't alone in their prudishness. The pagan philosopher Plotinus, for instance, was ashamed of his body to the point that he never disclosed details about his parents or birth. In the world of late antiquity the spiritual was vastly superior to the physical, the rational vastly superior to the emotional. And sex, of course, was strikingly and inextricably connected to the physical and emotional.

One church father in particular passed on this legacy. Augustine's influence in the Roman Catholic Church is unequaled. And the Protestant Reformers Calvin and Luther depended more heavily on him than any other father. So it is fair to get more specific by paying close attention to the sexual views of Augustine.

If Augustine was the profound Dr. Ruth of early Christianity, there is no danger of mistaking his views with those of our contemporary Dr. Ruth. Our Dr. Ruth delights in sexual arousal of many sorts. Not so Augustine. Sexual arousal of any kind deeply disturbed this great African churchman. But why? Because sexual desire, so intense and spontaneous, refuses to bow to its superiors: mind and will. People cannot control the arousal (or lack of arousal) of their sexual organs.

Ask any teenage boy who has taken a date to the movies and after heavy kissing has suddenly been asked to go for popcorn. Conveniently or not, the sexual organs do as they will when they will it. To Augustine this was the supreme example of "another law at war with the law of my mind, making me captive to the law of sin that dwells in my members" (Rom 7:23). Augustine read the Genesis texts of shame over nakedness and assumed the sexual organs were covered because they were out of control, unpredictable, beyond the rein of rationality.

Accordingly, he idealized virginity as the remastery of the rebellious body by a controlling mind and will. Sexual intercourse remained necessary for propagating the human race. But since it was always attended by the sin of lust, it ought to be practiced only for the purpose of conceiving a child, and even then the enjoyment of it ought to be resisted. Those who chose celibacy chose the morally and spiritually higher way. Begetting and rearing children were "duties," Augustine wrote, but "virginal integrity and freedom from all carnal relations through holy chastity is an angelic lot, and a foretaste in the corruptible flesh of perpetual incorruption." More bluntly, he declared, "Fertility is a blessing in marriage, but [virginal] integrity in holiness is better."

Eleven centuries later, Luther would revalue marriage and rank it above celibacy. His earthiness could even prompt him to encourage marriage for largely sexual reasons: "Stop thinking about it and go right to it merrily. Your body demands it. God wills it and drives you to it." But, though he softened it, Luther retained Augustine's interpretation of lust and the Genesis texts. He speculated, "In paradise, where there was no such ardor and raging passion, marriage must have been very pleasant. Flesh and blood were different then." He persisted in seeing the marriage act as "naturally impure."

As archaic as this view of sexual passion now seems, it has remained a strong undercurrent in Christian thought and morals long past the days of Augustine and the Reformation. In Victorian England it mutated and took the form of a double standard. Women, at least, would not enjoy sex. So the distinguished surgeon William Acton advised that "a modest woman seldom desires any sexual gratification for herself. She submits to her husband only to please him; and, but for the desire of maternity, would far rather be relieved of his attention."

For evidence of more recent vintage consider chapter five of C. S. Lewis's *The Problem of Pain.* There Lewis speculates that before the Fall, the primeval man's mind and spirit enjoyed total mastery of all bodily organs and drives. "His organic processes obeyed the law of his own will, not the law of nature. His organs sent up appetites to the judgment seat of the will not because they had to, but because he chose." If Lewis stands on the speaker's platform, Augustine clearly whispers cues from behind the curtain.

He does not explicitly mention sex, but Lewis imagines that in a perfect world the will and mind would control our organs and appetites. It is hard to see how such an attitude can avoid a fundamental suspicion of sex, an appetite that comes and goes unbidden by the will. A more modern attitude, and one now adopted by even the most conservative Christians, is that there is nothing at all impure about sexual attraction or, indeed, the involuntary activity of our sexual organs. How we respond to sexual attraction, whether or not we act on it, *is* an issue to be submitted to mind and will. But we need not feel guilty or ashamed because we are sexually aroused, and we should wholeheartedly enjoy sex within marriage. From this angle Augustinians are too concerned about the will's mastery; they are in that respect "control freaks."

None of this is to say we have outlived Augustine's monumental wisdom. His psychology of sexuality still addresses our frequent sense of alienation from ourselves. And surely sexual love rates among the most tempestuous and potentially dangerous of all human loves; it *can* foster self-absorption and even become demonic. But careful biblical exegesis simply does not support Augustine's reading of Genesis 2—3 (or Romans 7:21-25). As Walter Brueggemann comments on the Genesis story, "To find in this any focus on sex or any linkage between sex and sin is not faithful to the narrative." The point of nakedness here is vulnerability arising from the breach of trust—between Adam and Eve, and between them and God. With trust broken, Adam and Eve no longer feel safe to disclose themselves. The issue is not control over their sexual organs. Ironically, the issue is that Adam and Eve become control freaks. They want to hold total control over themselves, since they no longer feel secure to grant control to one another or even God.

This locates a wrong turn way, way back on the long road of Christian history. If the New Testament sees celibacy and singleness as permissible and even admirable, it is not because it sees sex as impure. It offers no real support for Augustine's suspicion of "carnal relations" and his exaltation of "virginal integrity." So if we are to recover the dignity and integrity of singleness for our day, we will need a clearer understanding of the New Testament's reasons.

Why the Childless Were Without Joy in Zion

In the matter of singleness as in so many other things, the New Testament's reasons have a background in the Old Testament. And the Old Testament provides no real place for single people. Even ascetics such as the priests and the Nazirites were not single (Lev 21:1-15; Num 6:1-21). In fact, for a Hebrew not getting married was catastrophic. So Isaiah has seven women pursuing one man, pleading, "We will eat our own bread and wear our own clothes; just let us be called by your name; take away our disgrace" (4:1). Blessing, in the Old Testament, means

bountiful crops, thriving community—and many children. A man's or
woman's life was simply incomplete if he or she did not marry and
procreate. Needless to say, there were no bachelor jokes in ancient
Israel. In fact, as we have noted, marriage was so taken for granted that
biblical Hebrew has no term for "bachelor."

There is more than one reason for this. A crucial and more familiar
reason is one we have already explored. Family is a sign and channel
of God's covenant with Israel. So the prophets repeatedly use marriage
as a metaphor of the covenant (for example, Is 50:1; Jer 3:1, 7-8; Ezek
16:23). God's blessing of the entire earth would spread through childbearing (Gen 12:2-3; 15:5; 22:17; and, from centuries later, Hos 1:10).
And of course the hoped- and yearned-for Davidic Messiah would one
day be birthed by a blessed mother and father.

But there is another and less familiar reason for the importance of
the family. Stranger to our contemporary Christian ears is the fact that
the Hebrews did not have a highly developed notion of the afterlife.
Following Greek and medieval Christian thought, we often sharply
separate the soul and body, and emphasize that the individual soul
survives death. What's more, we tend to believe the disembodied soul
has escaped to heaven, to a more pleasant and fully alive existence.

But we interpret anachronistically if we read this attitude back into
the Old Testament. There Job compares the dead person to a cloud that
"fades and vanishes" (7:9; see also Is 14:9-10; 26:14). With this gauzy,
pallid view of the person after death, the Hebrews referred to the dead
as the "shades" (Ps 88:10). In a careful evangelical treatment of the
matter, theologian John Cooper concludes that for the Israelites the
afterlife "is hopelessly pale and dull" in comparison to a blessed and
full earthly life. Sheol, the resting place of the dead, is "the Pit."

Deep down, it is as far away as one can get in the Israelite world-pic-
ture from the heaven of heavens, the dwelling place of God. And it

is hidden from the green earth, the realm of God's dealings with humankind. Not surprisingly, it is a place of deep darkness and gloom, cut off from the light. Its atmosphere is damp and dank, slimy and foul. Sheol has gates and bars which prevent those who enter it from escaping. It is a prison with many rooms and beds.

Existence in Sheol, Cooper continues, is characterized by "overpowering lethargy" and a "generally comatose condition." The dead in Sheol were usually unconscious, though "on occasion they could become conscious and active."

But what does all this mean for singleness? Simply this: Treading in the path of medieval Christianity, we may have no trouble imagining life after death for the single person. Indeed, we (mistakenly) envision the Christian hope as an individual affair, a matter of separate souls taking flight to heaven. But none of this was the case for the ancient Israelites. For the Hebrews, survival after death was primarily a matter of handing on the family name, especially through the eldest son. The name was no mere label. It expressed the essential nature and character of its bearer, which is why the pious yearned to know the name of God (Ps 9:11; 91:14). True enough, the individual existed after death, in some way, in Sheol. But a more vital existence continued among the living, on the "green earth" and nearer to the "heaven of heavens."

In its concern for the individual's connection to a family, the Israelite's life bears comparison to a campfire. Separate twigs and branches burn to ashes and fade, but the family fire blazes on if more twigs and branches follow the earlier ones. So, as the Old Testament scholar Johannes Pedersen summarized it,

> the house bears the name of the father of the house, and this implies that his soul [that is, his essential or characteristic self] imbues the whole of the family with everything that belongs to it. After his death the name is taken over by the son; it means that he does not die. His

soul, with all its substance, great achievements, wealth, blessing, honour, everything which fills the name, lives on in the son.

This is why, for the Hebrew, nothing is worse than the extermination of the name through failure to bear children (as in Num 27:4; 1 Sam 24:22; 2 Sam 14:7; Ruth 4:10).

The Superiority of Singleness for Awkward Times

The picture changes dramatically in the New Testament. There are only hints of resurrection from the dead in the Old Testament (as in Dan 12:1-4), but by Jesus' time resurrection was a widespread Jewish expectation. And for Christians, of course, this hope was solidified and vividly confirmed in Jesus' own resurrection.

It is in the light of Jesus and his resurrection that Paul can write, "He who marries his fiancée does well; and he who refrains from marriage will do better" (1 Cor 7:38). For Paul, Jesus' career, death and resurrection marked the end of the old age and the beginning of the new age (1 Cor 10:11; Gal 4:4). And the new age made all things new, including marriage. Jesus' resurrection brought about nothing less than an epochal shift for marriage and singleness. The rabbis of Jesus' day saw marriage as a moral and religious duty: to be unmarried at the age of twenty was to transgress a commandment of God. But in the new age Jesus heralded, marriage was no longer a duty (Mt 19:10-12). With the coming of the kingdom, as we saw in chapter four, natural family relationships were made secondary in doing the will of God.

Paul, the great apostle of Christian freedom, exploited this new liberty. He saw that both singleness and marriage were now honorable vocations to be lived out in service to God. He valued and could esteem as a "gift" both the call to remain single and the call to marry (1 Cor 7:7, 17-24). So in exactly what sense did he consider singleness "better"?

No less than Jesus, Paul recognized that the new age does not come painlessly. It is not accepted serenely. Jesus announced and embodied God's kingdom; the church after him witnesses to this Lord and his kingdom. But this means that all false gods and idols are challenged. The rule of the powers and the principalities—the undue, overreaching claims of governments, markets, fashions, cultures, educational and other institutions—is revealed to be illegitimate and ultimately destructive. So the false gods are not friendly to Jesus and those who would worship only the God he called Father. And so we live in awkward times. The new age has begun but is not here in its fullness; the old age drags on with more than a little effect and efficiency. Because the powers of the old age remain real and often malignant, Christians can survive only with hope—the hope of Jesus' return and the complete manifestation of God's loving, just rule.

This is the context of Paul's counsel in 1 Corinthians 7. Because Jesus has come and will return to fulfill or complete his rule, we live in a time of distress and crisis (vv. 26, 29). The world's possessions, joys and business have been revealed for what they are. They are good, but they are not ultimately good, because they are "passing away" (v. 31). In 1 Corinthians 7, Paul seems to recognize at least two things.

First, since Christians pray and strive to live in the light of the new age and the one God it reveals, they will be swimming against the current of the old age and its many gods. Life will be wearisome. And sometimes it will be perilous, because the gods of the old age will lash out in persecution.

Second, Paul recognizes that the married person is likely to sink more deeply into the affairs of the passing world (v. 33). With spouse and children, the married person takes on additional responsibilities and anxieties. I think, for instance, of an opportunity I had some years back. A relief agency needed a journalist who would travel around the world and write stories about needy peoples and countries. It was an attractive and worthy job, but I thought of leaving my wife and child several weeks out of every month and decided not to apply. By contrast, a single and "unencumbered" friend quickly submitted his application. The married must think not only of themselves and God's call for them, but also of what that call will mean for spouse and children. Family does complicate things.

This is how and why singleness is "better" in Paul's eyes. Understandably enough, he wants those he cares about to be as free as possible of worry (v. 32). But he explicitly says marriage is not a sin (v. 28). The single, celibate Christian is not holier or more moral than the married, sexually active Christian. What Paul offers is practical counsel for living in the awkward time between the times. The single Christian will live and serve in less complicated "devotion to the Lord" (v. 35).

Thus we can avoid what might be called the "old-fashioned," or Augustinian, misinterpretation of this text. Virginity is no great and saintly virtue in and of itself. Sexual activity is not inherently corrupting. But we should also avoid what could be called the "new-fangled" misinterpretation of the text. The modern misinterpretation correctly sees there is nothing sinful about sex, that it is indeed a great good and can be enjoyed. But the modern misinterpretation incorrectly proceeds to imagine that the most important thing the celibate person gives up is sex. Ironically, both the old-fashioned and the new-fangled views are sex-obsessed. The old-fashioned is obsessed with sex because it sees sex as uniquely corrupted. The new-fangled is obsessed with sex because it sees sex as utterly necessary to any full and happy life.

What both the old-fashioned and the new-fangled views overlook is Paul's Old Testament and Jewish context, with its consuming concern for heirs to the family name. Paul recognizes the existence and intensity of the sexual drive (see vv. 1-9), yet from his cultural vantage point, as theologian Stanley Hauerwas writes, "the 'sacrifice' made by the single is not that of 'giving up sex,' but the much more significant sacrifice of giving up heirs." Without children, the Israelite fears the single's name will burn out, sift to ashes and be scattered and forgotten in the winds of time. But Paul has seen the arrival of a new hope. Jesus has risen from the land of death and forgetfulness, and so someday shall all who have died. And Jesus has inaugurated the kingdom, a kingdom most fundamentally known and seen not among brothers and sisters in kin, but among brothers and sisters in Christ. Thus Hauerwas says of single-ness, "There can be no more radical act than this, as it is the clearest institutional expression that one's future is not guaranteed by the family, but by the church. The church, that harbinger of the Kingdom of God, is now the source of our primary loyalty."

The married Christian ultimately *should* trust that his or her survival is guaranteed in the resurrection; the single Christian ultimately *must* trust in the resurrection. The married, after all, can fall back on the passage of the family name to children, and on being remembered by children. But singles mount the high wire of faith without the net of children and their memory. If singles live on, it will be because there is a resurrection. And if they are remembered, they will be remembered by the family called church.

Christian singles are thus radical witnesses to the resurrection. They forfeit heirs—the only other possibility of their survival beyond the grave—in the hope that one day all creation will be renewed. The Christian single life makes no sense if the God of Jesus Christ is not living and true.

The Odd Freedom of the New Testament

Now we are in a position to appreciate the genuine, full freedom that Christian singleness points to. Our market-oriented culture promotes the illusion of the autonomous individual. In that setting freedom is understood negatively, as liberation from commitments, burdens, identities or histories that would limit options. Freedom is uncurtailed choice, the ability to "shop" for everything from mouthwashes to churches.

Christian singleness radically witnesses to a very different kind of freedom. The New Testament agrees with contemporary culture in seeing slavery as a matter of being controlled or possessed by something outside ourselves. Thus, from its viewpoint, we can be slaves to money (Mt 6:24), passions and appetites (Tit 3:3), and sin and death (Rom 6:16-23). But the New Testament does not imagine such a thing as an autonomous person. Everyone is under the influence of and belongs to one god or another—even if it is a god no more glorious than one's own belly (Phil 3:19). So freedom is not utter independence or uncurtailed choice. Instead, freedom is dependence on and decision for the one true, living God (Jn 8:35-36; Rom 6:16-23; 7:6; 1 Pet 2:16). New Testament freedom is freedom *from* money, appetites, passions, sin, death and other false gods, but it is even more significantly freedom *for* the service of God (Gal 5:13).

The modern ideal of liberation is one of casting aside custom, tradition and social inhibition to decide for ourselves, moment by moment, who we will be and what we will do. A Christian critique of this version of freedom must ask how much of a self will be left if individuals are cut off from the past and from responsible relationship to others—especially to God.

The Christian single radically witnesses to the truth for all of us: outside of relationship to God and others, we are lost. We do not know who we are, and we have no real assurance of an identity beyond death. In the biblical tradition no one gets at the "essence" of the human self by trying to determine what a human being is in isolation, as an individual removed from all community. Israel knows itself in relation to God: its very name means "God-wrestler" (Gen 32:28). Who is an

Israelite? An Israelite is a member of the people who are engaged by and struggle with the God of Abraham, Jacob and Moses.

Jesus says something similar when he declares, "Those who want to save their life will lose it" (Mk 8:35). We will not find our real selves by holding on to and hoarding the "autonomous" selves we have tried to create. Instead, we must give up these lesser, false selves to the higher and truer purposes of God. As Calvin put it, "In knowing God, each of us also knows himself." Or as a recent Orthodox theologian writes in the same vein, " 'Know yourself' means 'know yourself as God-sourced, God-rooted; know yourself in God.' "

From this perspective, modern "autonomous" and "liberated" individuals are little more than lonely amnesiacs without country, tribe or faith. They are doomed, like Fitzgerald's Jay Gatsby, to row a tiny, isolated boat "ceaselessly away from shore." And they are blind to what, in the end, can be the most confining and certainly destructive slavery of all—slavery to the unchecked but confused and lost self. After all, we can be rescued from terrorists, delivered from the whip of the slave master in Egypt or on the Georgia plantation, freed from Auschwitz. But no commando, no Moses or Lincoln, no Allied soldier can rescue or free us from ourselves. The New Testament knows what modern wisdom forgets: my ultimate enemy lives inside my skin, draws breath with my selfsame lungs.

The New Testament ideal of liberation calls the individual away from isolated self into community, away from amnesia to memory, away from an aimless future to destiny. As merely discrete selves, we are in fact a cacophonous, barely coherent collection of drives, impulses, whims and ill-formed dreams. We are little more than the child who wants one day to be a firefighter, the next to be a police officer, the third to be a doctor. To become a self of some unity and persistence over time, we need a cause or loyalty bigger than ourselves. With that cause or loyalty we have something to focus half-baked hopes, something to discipline our appetites and judge our competing desires. From it we derive motivation and strength for constancy and steadiness, and through constancy we develop a real self, an identity, a personhood with particular and enduring characteristics. Seen from this perspective, self is not something we create. It is something we discover, and so something that has been given. It is, in other words, a calling.

Put in biblical terms, we are liberated through Christ's death and resurrection to become servants of the kingdom. This is our cause, our loyalty, our calling. This is the discovery of what we really are: we are creatures made by God, intended for his service and the service of other creatures. But our service is not a matter of compulsion, as with slavery to the passions and appetites; or of coercion, as with slavery to merely human masters or causes; or of fearful leverage, as with slavery to sin and sin's threat of death. Rather, it is responsible service—service chosen in response to the loving and graceful work of God in Christ. Thus we are free and use that freedom to serve all (1 Cor 9:19). We discover who we truly are, creatures of God gifted with one another. And this is our destiny or calling, the freedom of service that binds us to one another and enriches our lives.

Ours is a freedom so great that Paul cannot contain it entirely within the metaphor of servanthood. So he tells us we are no longer slaves but family members, sons and daughters, heirs of God, and the adopted siblings of Jesus (Gal 4:1-7). Paul's text is especially rich in light of both Jewish and Roman customs. He writes that heirs, "as long as they are minors, are no better than slaves; . . . they remain under guardians and trustees until the date set by the father" (vv. 1-2). In the Hebrew and Roman worlds, slaves came under the guardianship and might even be given the name of their master-father. But they could make no real claims against that name. They were not, for instance, entitled to an inheritance. Nor would they be considered true and full representatives of that name; that privilege belonged to the father and, to some extent, the eldest son.

Consequently, slaves and underage or minor heirs were directed by guardians and trustees. But now, Paul writes, we have through Christ attained our majority, been granted full adoption and control over the inheritance (vv. 4-7). The family name or identity is ours, and we are its full representatives. In other words, we have been given selfhood (name, identity) and are now responsible for it. What we do and become with it is no longer mediated by guardians or trustees of any kind (v. 3).

All Christians, but singles most acutely, are signs of the genuine freedom and ennobling responsibility available to us through Christ the elder brother. They are invitations to full membership, with all privileges, in first family, the blessed community we call church.

The Variety of Christian Freedoms

Single Christians, then, are our most radical witnesses to the variety of genuine, profound Christian freedoms.

Not least of these is *freedom from biological compulsion.* The provocative neopagan Camille Paglia is exactly right when she claims, "Modern psychology, following Rousseau, pessimistically roots sex deeper than does Judeo-Christianity, which subordinates sex to moral will. Our sexual 'freedom' is a new enslavement to ancient Necessity." Indeed, our culture tends to consider the sexual drive undeniable, so much so that some suggest condom distribution in elementary schools. The main counsel about AIDS prevention, for unmarried teens and adults, has been "safe sex." Abstinence is considered "unrealistic" at best.

Christianity, in contrast, sees genital expression as something that can and should be disciplined. Our sexuality can be unified with the rest of our selves and our purpose in life. A true self will never be found by simply surrendering to drives and impulses. We are not enslaved to our genitals, and genital expression is ideally reserved for marriage.

Furthermore, to live without genital expression is not to be less than a whole person. Our popular and commercial media relentlessly insist that sex will make our lives complete. Early Christians were seen as atheists because they rejected the proposition that Caesar saves. Late-twentieth-century Christians would be little less revolutionary in their "atheism" if they now rejected the proposition that sex saves. And what bolder way to reject that proposition than to live a full and vigorous life without sex?

Single Christians, ironically, are also our most vivid witnesses to the *freedom to marry*. The ancient Israelites were not free to remain single. Singleness, in a real way, was synonymous with death and extinction. But we are now truly free to be single, and so truly free to be married. In the power of Christ and his resurrection, we can now count as calling and gift our single state or our married state; in either we can serve God (1 Cor 7:7, 17, 20, 24).

It has been too easy for the Christian community to forget that *both* marriage and singleness are vocations. The church has often seen marriage as automatic and reflexive. Ordinarily, you grow up and get married. Those who do not are then necessarily considered odd. They are single by default.

But this is the wrong picture. In the church, by virtue of Christ's death and resurrection, singleness is of equal status to marriage. Those of us with children should not simply assume our sons or daughters will one day marry. Our young people should be *Christianly* counseled, and that means they should be counseled to seriously consider whether or not they are called to marriage. If they are, all to the good. But if they are not, all to the good as well. Their lives will have no less meaning, present no fewer opportunities for service. In the church singles are not spare wheels. Christian marrieds need singles no less than singles need marrieds. If we are not truly free to be single, we are not truly free to be married.

The Christian freedoms of singleness and marriage are, in other words, complementary. And this complementarity has some quite practical effects. One of them has to do with parenting. Christian parenting is a task for the entire church. It is a responsibility even for those who have never conceived or legally adopted a child. I am not disputing the *primacy* of the biological or adoptive parents. Tradition and, increasingly, contemporary science show that children flourish when one or two particular adults consistently nurture them. But, as I have argued throughout the pages of this book, Christian parents are agents of the church. And they are engaged in a task too big and important for them alone. Single Christians should not be exempt from either the joys or the responsibilities that children bring. Singles are significant role models. And in a transient society where many children are separated from biological relatives by hundreds of miles, singles can serve invaluably as surrogate grandparents or aunts and uncles. (A service most important, of course, to the parent without a spouse.)

Another aspect of the complementarity of single and married Christians is at least hinted at in 1 Corinthians 7. We have noted that without the intimate ties and primary responsibilities to spouse and children, the single has fewer "hindrances" in the world. So we might say that singles and marrieds have complementary missionary advantages. The married Christian has the missionary advantage of hospitality (a point I will expand in the following chapters). The single Christian has the missionary advantage of mobility. I don't mean to say that the Christian single should be willing to pick up and leave job and home at any time or any request. Singles have ties and responsibilities too, and these are not trivial. But on balance it is simpler for the single, should it seem right, to move into a new situation, to make do with less money or even to confront potentially dangerous circumstances. This is not something for married Christians to exploit: no Christian, whether married with children or not, is exempt from moving, giving up possessions or facing danger. Yet singles themselves can affirm a unique missionary advantage and take it seriously. This, too, can be part of their freedom in Christ.

The Christian single witnesses to a third freedom, the *freedom to be a whole self rather than a schizophrenic self.* Psychologist Kenneth Gergen has noted that the postmodern personality is bombarded with choices. And we confront choices from an increasing number of sources—not just radio, TV and the telephone, but now also faxes and computers. Gergen sees the threat of a besieged, overpopulated self spiraling into "multiphrenia."

To put it in more conventional terms, schizophrenia is *the* malady of the postmodern age. Schizophrenia in fact excellently serves the purposes of consumer capitalism. If, as we have observed, heaven is a supermarket, I should live as if I have no history, no persisting identity that might bind me to a particular commitment and so at a later point stifle the pursuit of a new want or need. The affluent schizophrenic is the perfect shopper.

But schizophrenia is, of course, dysfunctional. The clinically schizophrenic man or woman is the ultimately private person, someone "free" of the norms and reality affirmed by a wider community, and "free" of an identity and all the commitments and ties an identity entails. A schizophrenic can choose anything—even the "real world" he will inhabit tomorrow. But as a consequence he gives up a persisting identity, a unified and genuine self. The schizophrenic is not only alone. In the world outside his head, a world inhabited by other people, he is paralyzed and impotent.

We have seen, by contrast, that the gospel points to a true freedom.

It offers a story, a cause and loyalty, to enliven and organize our dreams, to focus and discipline our drives, our impulses, our whims. It fosters a community of shared and not merely private reality, where gifts are complementary and used for the common good. Surely this is what we need to escape the "tyranny of choice," to achieve a somewhat integrated and whole self. And the lives of single Christians are our most radical signs of the hope that real selfhood is based on the kingdom revealed in the work, death and resurrection of Jesus Christ.

Single Christians are signs of another, and similar, freedom. It is the *freedom to enjoy positive freedom as well as negative freedom.* We have observed that freedom in our culture has been understood negatively, as freedom *from* restrictions, ties, commitments. But this ironically leaves us unfree to choose and embrace positive freedom, freedom *for* something. With such a misguided ideal, we can only exercise freedom when we act destructively—when we quit one brand of peanut butter for another, when we leave a relationship or abandon a child.

Christian freedom is not only negative and destructive, but positive and constructive. It frees us from sin and death, but not so that we can simply be left alone. Instead, it frees us to live with and for others. It frees us to become and remain spouses and parents. It frees us to become and remain friends. And in a postmodern world of growing choices and equality for women, of shifting sex roles, we perhaps need help to be friends in no area more than friendship between the sexes.

As contemporary psychology has rightly reminded us, abstention from genital sex does not mean the end of sexuality. Men and women relate sexually on many levels. But our culture (partly because of the influence of a misguided Christianity) has been impoverished in recognizing this. Men and women have been taught to see one another only in the most starkly contrasting, black-and-white terms: either as lovers or as the most casual of acquaintances. But no longer are male and female domains so neatly and tightly separated between the public, or work, world and the private, or domestic, world. More than in the past, men and women must learn to see each other not only as lover or acquaintance but also as colleague, supervisor, employee. And no longer are single people content to pretend they are somehow asexual.

All this can threaten. Indeed, it does unsettle old and stable arrangements—the woman at home with children, the man in a workplace mainly populated by other men. And when men and women are together, feelings inevitably arise. Among other things, affairs can happen. But the church should be at the forefront of recognizing and affirming the complex richness of human sexuality. After all, our faith confesses that realizing the image of God means appreciating the complementarity of the sexes, for we are created male and female (Gen 1:27). Relationships between men and women can never be entirely "safe," but following Jesus is not about being safe. And even if it were, there is good reason to doubt that rigid separation of sexes effectively prevents extramarital sex. Such separation serves only to reinforce the impoverished, overly narrow idea that a member of the other sex can be only a love object or a casual acquaintance. When people saddled with such cramped imaginations have any feelings at all for a woman or man, they are faced with only two options: go to bed or never see each other again. This isn't freedom. This is tragedy.

Thus we need to expand our imagination and affirm the possibility and practice of cross-sexual friendships, both between singles and by married Christians welcoming singles into their lives. I mean this not only in the workplace but also in our homes and churches. As Lewis Smedes writes, "A covenant-keeper does not have to worry much or moralize a great deal about the proprieties of relationships outside marriage. Within commitment there is room for surprises, risks, and adventures. Loyalty is limiting but not constricting."

Our lives and our witness in the world are enriched when we welcome, learn from and enjoy Christian siblings from other cultures. It is time to recognize that welcoming, learning from and enjoying Christian siblings of the other sex is itself an enriching "crosscultural" experience. Fellowship across racial lines is a witness to Christ's reconciliation of the peoples from all nations. Fellowship across sexual lines challenges the antagonism between men and women, the enmity and suspicion so often apparent in clashes over women's liberation. It, too, can be a profound witness to Christ's reconciliatory power.

Finally, I believe single Christians can especially embody another freedom, the *freedom to acknowledge and live within limits.* The modern world was a world oblivious to limits. The individual was supposedly autonomous, able to create his or her world and self. Capitalism, born in modernity, thrives on the hope of limitless economic growth. And historian Christopher Lasch has argued that the central modern myth was the myth of progress: even if there is no heaven above, life here on earth will get infinitely better and better.

But one of the paradoxes of a postmodern world is that at the same time choice has proliferated as never before, we are becoming acutely aware of certain limitations. The ozone layer deteriorates, the greenhouse effect threatens, and we realize the earth cannot tolerate unlimited pollution and abuse. The economy seems to have peaked, and for the first time in American history a generation of youth anticipates not being materially better off than their parents. Apparently there are limits to economic growth.

With a negative understanding of freedom and under the modern myth of progress, limits can only be seen as a curse. Once more, a Christian vision presents an alternative. Like other visions of constructive freedom, the Christian tradition recognizes that true freedom admits limits—and even takes on new limits such as wedding vows.

In his memoirs, John Updike surprisingly devotes an entire chapter to his psoriasis. Why?

Whenever in my timid life I have shown some courage and originality it has been because of my skin. Because of my skin, I counted myself out of any of those jobs—salesman, teacher, financier, movie star—that demand being presentable. What did that leave? Becoming a craftsman of some sort, closeted and unseen—perhaps a cartoonist or writer, a worker in ink who can hide himself and send out a surrogate presence, a signature that multiplies even while it conceals.

My point, of course, is not to compare singleness (or marriage) to a skin disease. It is to recognize that one of our best living writers became a writer—had the call to be a writer—because of a mundane condition, a humbling limitation. Most likely any of us would need only a little reflection to see that many of the things we most prize about ourselves owe something to limitations, givens, circumstances over which we had no say and may never have chosen, or other limitations that we did choose but that have proved to be more demanding and more rewarding than we first imagined.

Marriage and parenthood are chosen limitations. Singleness is for many Christians an unchosen limitation. Yet Paul can find freedom in the ordinary, nitty-gritty qualities of all these limitations: Are you single? Then live as a Christian in that state. Are you married? Then live as a Christian in that state. Are you a slave? Are you circumcised or uncircumcised? "In whatever condition you were called, brothers and sisters, there remain with God" (1 Cor 7:24). For Paul, vocation is no towering mystery. It is simply the condition in which "you were called."

We cannot apply these words with wooden literalness and assume, for example, that someone converted at age fifteen should remain forever single. (Or, for that matter, that slavery is good and should never be abolished.) But we can recognize that God is able to meet us and enrich us in a variety of circumstances. I suspect too much has been made of the purported "gift of celibacy." Probably very few people—many fewer than the number who are actually Christian singles—have a hardly noticeable sexual drive. The more important point, as I have already indicated, is that the sexual drive is manageable. It is not compulsory, and a truly free appropriation of sexuality will not be compulsive. Of course the single life will include frustration and pain. But, as Paul recognizes, married Christians are not exempt from the same. And much of the frustration and pain of both singles and marrieds will be eased if together we learn that our first family is the church. Then, for instance, marrieds can soften the loneliness of the single, and singles can aid marrieds in the demanding task of parenthood. Within the community engendered by the kingdom of God, we can faithfully affirm a variety of calls and "conditions."

Indeed, it is our very conditions and limitations that turn us from fantasy and self-pity to the genuine freedom to be found in the actual circumstances of our lives. As long as we are "free" to abandon commitments or deny the liabilities of our condition, we need trust only our own meager resources. My life will be (only) what I make it. My talents will be developed merely to the threshold of frustration. Yet as Wendell Berry writes, "It may be that when we no longer know what to do we have come to our real work and that when we no longer know which way to go we have begun our real journey. The mind that is not baffled is not employed. The impeded stream is the one that sings."

To be free is to accept and respect the right limitations. Since the single Christians in our midst are among the most faithful and powerful witnesses of this truth, it is worth saying again: one sure sign of a defective interpretation of Christian family is that it denigrates and dishonors singleness.

CHAPTER SIX

―――

WHOSE FIDELITY?
WHICH INTIMACY?

•

Our bond is no little economy based on the exchange
of my love and work for yours, so much for so much
of an expendable fund. We don't know what its limits are—
that puts it in the dark. We are more together
than we know, how else could we keep on discovering
we are more together than we thought?
Wendell Berry, "The Country of Marriage"

Singles, we have seen, have a distinctive place and purpose in the
Christian story. But so do married women and men. Their Christian
distinctiveness was not so obvious thirty years ago, when lifelong
marital fidelity was a societywide ideal. It is more obvious now exactly
because our society no longer expects one man and one woman to
remain married for a lifetime.

In the United States in 1960, there were 35 divorced persons for
every 1,000 married persons. Today there are 142 for every 1,000,
which amounts to a 406 percent increase in three decades. Divorce is
now so common, so expected or predictable for such large numbers of
people, that our culture has ritualized it. Newspaper society pages
announce divorce parties. Lutherans, United Methodists and Episcopa-

lians are among the venerable denominations that currently offer divorce prayers and liturgies. Greeting-card companies manufacture divorce cards bearing messages like this one:

> Think of your marriage as a record album. It was full of music, both happy and sad. But what's important now is YOU: the newly released hot new single!

Calculation Never Made a Christian Spouse

What we must recognize is that these things make sense in a culture dominated by the market, living under an economic exchange model of reality and marriage. People change. New options present themselves. "Trading up" is a nuptial as well as an automotive possibility.

The odd title of this chapter ("Whose Fidelity? Which Intimacy?") echoes an important book by one of the most insightful philosophers of postmodernity, Alasdair MacIntyre. *Whose Justice? Which Rationality?* is MacIntyre's sophisticated reminder that there is more than one understanding of justice, more than one definition of what is reasonable. Ronald Reagan and George Bush believe justice is done when people get what they deserve; Jesse Jackson and Jimmy Carter believe justice is done when resources are equally distributed. Carl Sagan thinks rationality is served by listening first to science; John Calvin thinks rationality is served by listening first to Scripture. Likewise, Christians in a postmodern world are made vividly aware that there is more than one way to understand and practice marital intimacy, more than one way to interpret and live out fidelity.

After all, marriage itself is not dying in our culture. Most people who divorce sooner or later remarry. But fidelity isn't dying either. Divorced people, even those who are divorced more than once, are still pursuing a certain kind of faithfulness, even if it is nothing more than faithfulness to the quest to achieve the perfect marriage. No, marriage and fidelity are not dying. What may be dying is *Christian* marriage; it is *Christian* fidelity that is in peril.

It's as if two bridge-builders were given separate blueprints and went to work. One builds a bridge that stands tall and supports traffic for generations. The other builds a bridge that is extraordinarily attractive, but after a few years collapses. Both builders were honest, decent, well-meaning people. Both started out with about the same skills and materials. The difference was that they built according to different plans. Whose blueprints? Which bridge?

But take it a step further. With inquiries, we learn the builder of the collapsed bridge never meant it to carry traffic. He intended to construct an impressive sculpture. The people who drove their cars across it were using it as it was never meant to be used. So the complexity and confusion deepens. Whose blueprints? Which bridge? *What for?* Marriage built according to the economic exchange model is simply not intended to serve the same aims and ends as Christian marriage.

In Christendom, a world where Christians dominated, monogamous and lifelong marriage seemed natural—the self-evidently best way to practice marriage. But Christendom has passed, and now we can see that lifelong monogamy is not self-evidently best to any and every rational, decent human being.

In fact, in some circles it is seen as self-evidently absurd and certainly impossible. I am not talking about exotic marriage in some distant land, like that of nomadic Arab Muslims, nor of some easily ignored fringe group (like a few traditionalist, polygamous Mormons). Christian covenantal fidelity does not make sense right here at home, in our consumer culture. This is sharply illustrated in Paul Mazursky's 1991 film *Scenes from a Mall.*

Mazursky's protagonists are Deborah and Nick, a Los Angeles couple married for sixteen years. The duration of their marriage sets

Deborah and Nick apart from their friends, none of whom has stayed in a single marriage nearly so long. And Nick and Deborah are all the more remarkable because they have been faithful to one another for all that time. Or so we think.

The film unfolds as Nick and Deborah spend the day at a mall, wandering from store to store, picking up anniversary presents, dining—and eventually confessing that they have each been involved in extramarital affairs. Along the way we hear the oft-quoted statistic that three-quarters of all American spouses cheat on one another. And we hear an eminent psychologist declare (in a bookstore videotape) that lifelong monogamy was once realistic—when people lived only to age thirty.

By setting his film in a shopping center, Mazursky can emphasize the centrality of "felt needs" in our culture, as well as the vast array of options available. He suggests that the mall is a microcosm of our entire world: we shop not only for cars and compact discs but also for friends and mates. And he suggests how rapidly people change in such a world: signaling an alteration of identity within hours, Nick and Deborah buy and don new clothes in the store, leaving their old garments behind.

Nick and Deborah, like most of us, are caught between two worlds. Christendom and its marriage and family norms lie within memory. Nick and Deborah want to adore one another forever; they want to enjoy and support their children together. Each has one foot (or maybe just a toe or two) in the world of Christendom. Yet in a consumer world these expectations seem increasingly strenuous and increasingly odd. With so much variety and possibility available, how can Nick and Deborah "restrict" themselves to one lover for a lifetime? How can either of them legitimately ignore his or her wants and needs, even "for the sake of the children," when doing so will prevent self-fulfillment, the achievement of real and whole personhood? Surely they would more wisely see their marriage as a partnership with carefully designated terms, a partnership efficiently terminated when the terms are no longer met—a kind of contractual fidelity.

Christian fidelity—monogamous, lifelong marriage—falters now because the church has not been sufficiently aware, first, that it has a distinctive "plan" or story for fidelity; and, second, that a different "plan" has been slipped onto the builder's desk. Our rightful plan for Christian marriage would lead us to the construction of *covenantal* fidelity. But there has been a switch, which we haven't adequately noticed, and for years we've mistakenly (if halfheartedly) gone along with a culture erecting marriages by the plan of *contractual* fidelity.

Covenantal fidelity is based on a promise. A man and woman promise one another, the church and God that they will be faithful to each other until death. Covenants are risky. They admit no qualifications or reservations. Husband and wife will love in sickness and in health, for better or for worse. For their marriage to succeed, they will have to rely on things bigger than themselves—God, the Christian community, the power of forgiveness and so forth.

Contractual fidelity is based on a calculation. A man and woman agree with one another that they will be faithful to each other unless one (or both) of them finds a better option. A contract is not so risky. It includes qualifications and reservations. It even anticipates how to handle the fallout if the marriage does break up. So there may be costs, losing the marriage may hurt, but it is a calculated risk.

Now I'm aware that, for all our talk about "unconditional" covenantal marriages, there really are circumstances when to dissolve a marriage is the lesser of evils. What about the chronically abusive husband? The automobile accident that leaves a spouse "vegetative" but breathing for years in a hospital? Teenagers swept into wedlock by passion, only to discover they really are incompatible everywhere other than the bed?

I can certainly imagine cases in which some marriages have become destructive, some divorces necessary, given the circumstances. That is part of what it means to live in a tragic world. But I do not think we should allow the exceptions, even legitimate exceptions, to define the rule. As Wendell Berry says, "The possibility of breaking a vow can tell us nothing of what is meant by making and keeping one." Trying to stay married by focusing on all the possibly legitimate reasons for divorce is like trying to stay healthy by imagining all the ways you might fall sick, or trying to attain wealth by studying the innumerable ways people slide into poverty.

Christian marriage remains covenantal, even if we sometimes fall short of this ideal. Christians undertaking the adventure of marriage must still make unconditional promises and *mean them.* John Henry Newman said calculation never made a hero. We might add that calculation never made a Christian spouse. But this is not an intuitively appealing view in our consumer culture, where we are taught to keep our options open. So we must understand all the better why Christians see monogamous, lifelong marriage as their ideal.

Postmodern Christian Fidelity

To put it in terms appropriate to postmodernity: *Married Christians live lives of fidelity so we can learn to recognize the God of faithfulness, the God of Israel and Jesus Christ.*

This is the truly strange thing about Israel. It was not chosen and rescued from Egyptian slavery because of its merit or great numbers. Instead, "it was because the LORD loved you and kept the oath that he swore to your ancestors, that the LORD has brought you out with a mighty hand, and redeemed you from the house of slavery" (see Deut 7:7-11). Through its history, its lived story, Israel comes to know the Creator God, the one and supreme Lord. And it learns that among the most important characteristics of this God are unyielding fidelity and unwavering grace. Yahweh is the "faithful God who maintains covenant loyalty" (Deut 7:9). This God's faithfulness "reaches to the clouds"; it is, in fact, God's "steadfast love" in practice (Ps 36:5; see also Ps 89). Eventually Israel comes to see monogamous marriage as a reflection of God's fidelity to Israel. The prophets (for instance, Hosea and Ezekiel) use faithful marriage as a picture of God's enduring, determined commitment to the chosen people, God's bride. Conversely, the prophets see promiscuity and prostitution as a reflection of Israel's infidelity. What we starkly notice in Israel's history (and later in the New Testament and the church's history) is the lack of faithfulness in God's people. God woos and weds, and even pursues a loved one who has fallen into whoredom, but Yahweh's people keep slipping away, betraying the trust, forming new allegiances, chasing other gods.

The same picture is picked up in the New Testament, most explicitly in Ephesians. There faithful, loving marriage is made a reflection of Christ's union with the church (Eph 5:31-32). Similarly, the book of Revelation sees the church and the renewed creation as Christ's bride, and imagines unfaithfulness as a kind of whoredom.

So the length and breadth of the Bible portrays a God who is faithful, but a people who are chronically unfaithful. Can the church today claim to be any more faithful, any less captivated by competing gods and cultural charms? Perhaps God is strangest and most foreign to us exactly here, in God's faithfulness. We are inclined to faithlessness. We flit from god to god, security to apparent security, thrill to thrill. The church and individual Christians constantly cozy up to ascendant ideologies and nationalisms. We are prone to prostitution, in the sense that we are constantly available to the highest bidder. Yet all the while the one and true God perseveres, keeps up wild pursuit of a beloved that will not be forgotten or relinquished.

I think fidelity *is* strange, more divine than human. And fidelity represents a particular kind of divinity. The Greek gods, after all, put no premium on loyalty to their people. Pagan divinity in general is not so much to be trusted as outwitted and manipulated. Fidelity is a mark, a key mark, of the God revealed to Israel—the God who chose, finally, to answer our betrayal with the cross rather than a flood of destruction. And so if we are to recognize and live in the light of this, the true divinity, we must strive to become the kind of people who practice at least enough faithfulness to know what it looks like.

This understanding of fidelity is postmodern because it recognizes that we all know and see from particular perspectives, and that there are things we can't actually know or see until we change our lives and adopt the appropriate perspective. Feminists present a strong postmodern insight when they worry that women who have had an abusive earthly father will have difficulty seeing their heavenly Father as a loving and benevolent reality. Evangelical Christians, feminists and nonfeminists, have similar concerns when they speak of "distorted images" of God. They counsel those who would see God truly to begin to live differently—read the Bible in a new light, participate in a loving church, get to know men who father well and so on.

Postmodernists understand that we can't see that slaves are oppressed until, at least figuratively, we walk in their shoes. We can't imagine that women deserve the vote until we have some experience that they, too, are political animals. We don't really know what it means to affirm Jesus as Lord until we follow him. So we must live lives of faithfulness to become the kind of people capable of recognizing the God who is faithful.

I know what faithfulness looks like because of people like Lee and Lester Imel, matriarch and patriarch in my home church, married nearly eighty years before Lester died. Theirs was a marriage of mutual admiration and respect, of love that had survived illness and poverty and the loss of a son to war. It was clear that this couple found depths of joy and meaning, in one another and their marriage, that could only be found through a lifetime of commitment.

I know what faithfulness looks like because I saw my mother stay faithful to her marriage vows, past the point my father was diagnosed with cancer, past the point of his depression, past the point of wiping up vomit and changing diapers, past the point where the vigorous and passionate man she had wed was a weak and skeletal shell of himself. She stayed, she stood, past all this to the point of death.

And I know what faithfulness looks like because so many people— Lester and Lee, my parents, my wife and a host of others—have held to vows explicit and implicit and, in the manner of their God, have been faithful to me. All this is what enables me, in my own small and poor way, to be faithful myself. It is a history, a personal story, that allows me to imagine that differences and adversity can be borne. It has bred into my bones the hope and courage that fidelity can last a lifetime, that people can be trusted enough for me to marry one of them. It answers the needs of my heart for assurance of continuing love and the opportunity, the possibility, to grow together in profound confidence and trust.

By contrast, I have friends born into tumultuous families, marriages riven by infidelity and so the tension of distrust. Of course my childhood and my own marriage have not been flawless; I struggle with the inability to trust, with a sometimes faltering faith in faithfulness. Yet again and again I have seen that the comparative peace and strength of my early models of marriage (as well as Sandy's) make it easier for me to trust, to hope that one mate will last me a lifetime, to believe that, ultimately, people were made to be faithful to one another. Not so the children of divorce: commitment is a fearsome thing to those who profoundly suspect it means opening themselves to inevitable betrayal and disappointment.

Without the confidence that promises can be made and kept, love must always be held back, restrained, guarded. What do I dare reveal to my wife if in three weeks or three years she may well be intimately involved with another man? How much of my life and resources do I commit to this marriage if it may end when the children grow up, or if an apparently more exciting and satisfying woman appears? Faithfulness undergirds love, at least the sort of love Christians are interested in. Without fidelity, the love that Paul sees as the crown and peak of human existence is impossible. Without fidelity, love cannot be patient, free of envy and boasting, able not to insist on its own way; it cannot bear and endure all things (1 Cor 13:4-7).

Fidelity as a Bodily Act

This is exactly the fidelity and love of the God of Israel and Christ. It is a fidelity and love we come to know through hearing *and living* the story of Israel and Christ. We must live it, because if we do not live it we cannot really hear it. If we do not live it, it will sound (if not to our ears, then to our children's) like incomprehensible nonsense, or a fairy tale, or the story for some ethereal, other-than-real world. But it is not that. It is a story for here and now; it is our quite physical world, according to the Christian story, that has been created and redeemed in the love of God. And that is why fidelity is a physical, bodily act.

With this we come to the famous Christian "obsession" with sex. Sooner or later all discussions of fidelity arrive at this crux. Why, after all, have Christians insisted on saving sex for marriage? Can't we loosen up, liberate ourselves a bit—at least, in an age of reliable birth control, can't we allow "consenting adults" a little freedom?

I suspect we do need to make some adjustments. The world has changed. But I do not believe we should abandon the strong Christian presumption for sex within marriage. On this count, at least, the church's problem is not that it is too heavenly-minded. Here it takes the body and sexuality more seriously than much of the world around it wants to take them. During the sixties it was popular to say sex is no more significant than drinking a glass of water. I thought this way of thinking had been discredited, but recently I heard it vigorously asserted again: sexual intercourse is recreational, and no more significant than holding hands.

This view is not new, which is to say it did not have to await the invention of modern birth control. Some Greeks in the apostle Paul's time thought sexual intercourse should be seen in the same light as eating and drinking. What you eat and drink is morally and religiously neutral—so, too, is sexual expression. Paul's Corinthian protégés thought this made eminent sense. Enjoying a wide latitude of sexual practices, they defended these to Paul by quoting a popular saying, "Food is meant for the stomach and the stomach for food," and concluding that God will one day destroy both (1 Cor 6:13). In other words, What's the big deal? The body and all its appetites will pass away. In the meantime, sex is no more significant than drinking a glass of water.

Paul had other ideas. Citing Genesis and Jesus, he reminded the Corinthians that sexual intercourse makes two people "one flesh" (1 Cor 6:16). True to his Jewish heritage, he saw the whole person as a unity of body and spirit. In sex we commit our body to another person. For Christians, then, there is no such thing as premarital or extramarital sex: all sex is marital, is the making of two into "one flesh."

So the problem with sex outside marriage is that it does not allow us to say with our spirits what we say with our bodies. With our bodies we say, "You and I are one, from now on." But we make no public promises; perhaps we even make no promises to one another. And so we are divided against ourselves. The body has committed itself, but the spirit has retained its options. (Or, colloquially speaking, the body is willing but the spirit is weak.) Only in marriage can we make love and remain whole. So in the Christian view, sex outside marriage is a betrayal of God and ourselves.

All this underscores the importance of fidelity not simply as an intellectual construct, as assent to a certain list of beliefs, but as the commitment and dedication of our entire selves—mind and body, spirit and flesh, alone and in community. Fidelity is what we think and imagine. Fidelity is what we feel. Fidelity is what we do with our bodies.

How Cohabitation Makes Sense

All this is true of Christian, covenantal fidelity. Calculated, contractual fidelity is another matter. Since it is the other "blueprint" so easily and so often slipped onto our drafting tables, we do well to return to it and learn more about recognizing it.

The contractual model of marriage commitment is tooled for an advanced capitalistic and market-dominated culture. It redesigns marriage along the lines of the business deal, seeing wedlock as a transaction between two self-interested partners—a transaction that, within certain conditions, will be mutually beneficial. And it assumes that once the transaction (the "deal") ceases to benefit either or both partners, it is legitimately nullified.

If you doubt the potency of contractual fidelity in our society, consider these three widespread phenomena:

1. The development of explicit prenuptial contracts. These contracts, carefully prepared by lawyers, designate privileges and liabilities in the event of a divorce. Often the people who draw up these contracts recognize that marriage has already been assumed to be contractual and wish only to make the contract more precise.

2. The unquestioned acceptance of no-fault divorce. This legal arrangement assumes that marriages, like business deals, sometimes just don't "work out." It makes no sense to assume that anyone must be blamed; for the good of both parties, the contract should be dissolved as painlessly and efficiently as possible. As scholar Lenore Weitzman writes, this arrangement has "shifted the focus of the legal process from moral questions of fault and responsibility to economic issues of pay and financial need."

3. The increase in couples living together before marriage. Corporations routinely try out one another with smaller deals before making long-term, riskier commitments. Why not potential spouses?

Now, the sort of fidelity giving rise to these developments is quite different from Christian fidelity. Covenantal fidelity, as I have said, is based on promises. In the classic marriage vows, spouses implicitly admit they have no idea what bliss or catastrophes lie ahead, but promise to stick together anyway. Years after the honeymoon, their marriage may face "worse" rather than "better," poverty rather than wealth, sickness rather health. That is beside the point. "In the Name of God," bride and groom unconditionally commit themselves to love and cherish one another until death.

Contractual fidelity sees this as reckless and imprudent. It emphasizes that circumstances are unforeseeable and that individuals change. *The Christian Century* records a recent blessing ceremony for homosexual couples. Here the lovers explicitly recognized their commitment as conditional. They pledged to pray and care for one another "as long as there is love." Closer to home, I think of a divorced friend. Her former husband insisted that in the fifteen years since their wedding he had "grown" and had become a "different person." He had no wish to blame or hurt my friend. But staying in his first marriage would now impede his continued growth. An understanding of marriage bounded by contractual fidelity put him in control of the circumstances and allowed him to depart a relationship he now defined as confining.

Notice, then, that contractual fidelity assumes the individual defines and determines marriage. It assumes the individual's wants and needs are fundamental. It also assumes the individual can understand his or her wants and needs better than any tradition, community or institution.

Covenantal fidelity starkly differs. It assumes marriage is bigger, deeper, older, wiser than any individual who enters into it. It sees marriage as a way of life that will itself shape and form individuals, will lead them to "grow" according to its gifts and demands. No one has expressed this more eloquently than the essayist Wendell Berry. Recognizing that covenantal marriage is given meaning and form by a specific community and tradition, Berry insists that "no one party to it can be solely in charge. What you alone think it ought to be, it is not going to be. Where you alone think it ought to go, it is not going to go. It's going where the two of you—and marriage, time, life, history, and the world—will take it. You do not know the road; you have committed your life to a way."

"You have committed your *life,*" Berry writes. Covenantal fidelity expects those who enter into it to hold nothing back. It aims at the unity of two selves. In Christian marriage, I commit my entire life and all its possibilities (as well as liabilities) to my spouse. This is at least something of what it means for two to become "one flesh" (Gen 2:24). No matter how much it disappoints me or burdens me, I cannot throw off my body and assume a new one. Likewise, covenantal fidelity expects my spouse and marriage to become an indispensable part of my identity, my very self.

Contractual fidelity, on the other hand, aims at a union of interests rather than a union of selves. Is this marriage aiding my growth, as I understand it? Is it helpful to my career, or at least not inhibiting it? Is it providing me sexual enjoyment, companionship, a comforting home life? All these are my interests. Contractual fidelity expects me to focus on them, to evaluate my marriage in the light of them. And it expects my spouse to do the same. A marriage should last exactly as long as it satisfactorily serves both spouses' interests.

Making Love, Making Persons

Clearly, then, covenantal fidelity and contractual fidelity are two different kinds of fidelity. Each shapes us into a particular kind of person. No one would be surprised by the suggestion that people become what they are intimate with. Consort with Nazis, and you are likely to become more and more like a Nazi. Join a socialist commune, and you will probably think and act increasingly like a socialist. Live in a middle-class American suburb, and your hopes and dreams will be those of middle-class American suburbanites.

But notice here that I am going a step further. A postmodern awareness shows us that we are shaped and changed not only by *whom* we are intimate with but by *how* we are intimate. Covenantal fidelity and contractual fidelity envision two contrasting sorts of intimacy, forming two different kinds of people.

Covenantal fidelity, as we have just seen, fosters an intimacy of selves; contractual fidelity fosters an intimacy of interests. Covenantal intimacy is unconditional—it rests on the promise and laying down of the spouses' whole lives, whatever circumstances follow. Contractual intimacy, based on interests rather than promise and selves, is conditional. In short, two kinds of intimacies, two kinds of persons molded from them.

The two intimacies locate persons in different arenas of account-ability and possibility.

Covenantal fidelity is the intimacy of two persons on a quest or adventure, something bigger than each of them individually or even both of them together. It is intimacy within a wider, supporting and correcting community, the church. ("Will all of you witnessing these promises do all in your power to uphold these two persons in their marriage?" the traditional Christian wedding liturgy asks.)

Contractual fidelity is the intimacy of two persons accountable only to him or herself. It is intimacy that disregards and rejects the authority of any community, seeking to serve only the ends of two people, the husband and the wife. In one sense it is less restricted, but in another sense it is limited to the possibilities of two people rather than the potential of an entire community.

The two intimacies shape persons with different purposes in life and so different ways of making love.

The ultimate aim of covenantal fidelity is intimacy with others through the individual self. This fidelity seeks to bind me to my spouse (and a community in service to God's kingdom). In covenantal fidelity, sex is a celebration of communion with another and the means of "creating" others who will live on and steward creation after me. In covenantal fidelity, the secure, stable love children need flows naturally and logically out of the relationship to the spouse. What is ultimately good for the marriage, my spouse and myself is also ultimately good for our children.

Contractual fidelity does not have the same ultimate aim. In it, the ultimate aim is intimacy with the individual self through others. Contemporary poet Bob Dylan portrays the kind of intimate relationship possible with such a grand and all-encompassing understanding of the self. In a classic popular song, Dylan admires a lover to the extreme: she is an "artist," someone who "never stumbles," has "everything she needs," stands beyond the law and even deserves worship. But what would appear to be unexcelled respect and admiration for the other is actually self-aggrandizement. The lover's real significance, the genuine importance of her extraordinary attributes, is betrayed by the song's title: "She Belongs to Me." Within the story told by contractual fidelity, intimacy with any one person, within any particular marriage, is valuable so long as it promotes my growth, enhances my status, fosters my self-fulfillment. In contractual fidelity, sex is a celebration of self and so finally a means of self-pleasuring, or masturbation. As for the children who may issue from lovemaking, they can easily be at odds with my narrowly described self-interest. Romance and career mobility are just two examples of the things children may hinder. And children achieve greater emotional health in a setting of security and stability. So children fit awkwardly at best into a contractual scheme of fidelity.

The two intimacies create persons with different kinds of histories or pasts.

Covenantal fidelity is intimacy with a particular story or history, the story of a specific woman and man who share a growing list of joys, who have endured trials and suffering unique to their marriage, their life together. The past matters. In fact, any one marriage or intimacy *is* its unique history, and so an intimacy that can be understood and told only as a story.

Contractual fidelity, on the other hand, is intimacy with no particular story or history. It is concerned with satisfaction or fulfillment from moment to moment. Guaranteed by no past promise and assured of no future, it lives only in the present and wants no story, no account of where it has been or where it is going.

The two intimacies make persons with different ways of relating and getting closer to others.

Covenantal fidelity assumes that intimacy is strengthened through complex commitment. Intimacy deepens as a couple's story lengthens, as they add yet another year of both trying and delightful episodes to their marriage. It is undergirded and enriched by continuing commitment, and so growing trust. Theirs is a *complex* commitment because it is the commitment of a particular man to a particular woman, so its life and success cannot be captured or explained in a "formula" applicable to any or all marriages. In fact, it cannot be captured or explained at all, but only recounted as a story, with parts or details that others may be able to appropriate and apply to their marriage.

Contractual fidelity, by contrast, assumes that intimacy is strengthened through technique. Do my spouse and I fight chronically and bitterly, hindering our intimacy? Then above all we need a seminar on conflict management. Is our sex lackluster? Give us a manual introducing us to new positions, better lovemaking methods. Are money worries ruining our marriage and our intimacy? Teach us how to redesign our budget, provide more effective investment strategies. Contractual intimacy assumes that marital commitment can be entirely submitted to the mechanics of the market. So of course it can be captured or explained by a "formula" applicable to any or all marriages. Contractual fidelity views marriages like machines, the people within them like interchangeable parts, their difficulties like mechanical breakdowns amenable to repair by technical experts.

Gridlock in Wheelchairs

By this time, nearing our chapter's end, it may seem I have executed a scorched-earth attack on the economic exchange model of marriage and fidelity. In fact, I have no doubt that a more sympathetic and generous portrait of contractual fidelity could be painted. But I believe what the church needs at the moment is a sharper awareness of its differences with the kind of marriage and persons created by the belligerent bottom line. Christians have too long and too zestfully remade our covenants in the image of the market.

And surely the stakes are high. A colleague of mine, a counselor, has over the years seen a steady increase of people who can only look out for their own interests, who were born of parents with the same limitations, and who live out of profound distrust and pain. He finds these people less and less capable of making allegiances to friends, to spouses, to children, to jobs, to churches, to their nation. Emotionally, he suggests, we may become a society of people in wheelchairs, severely restricted in our movement. We bang into each other and lock wheels, but can then only scream in anger and frustration at each other and the empty darkness.

Gridlock in wheelchairs. That may be the end result of a society of marriages and families built on the economic exchange model. One thing is certain: these marriages and families do not help make Christian communities and Christian persons. Whose fidelity? Which intimacy? These questions matter.

CHAPTER SEVEN

WELCOMING CHILDREN
& OTHER STRANGERS

•

When you're married and have your children, you will
know this: We don't have as much to do with our
young as we think. They do not come from us. They just
appear, as if they broke through a net of vines.
Once they live in our lives and speak our language,
they slowly seem to become like us.

Louise Erdrich, *Tracks*

Around the corner and down the way lives an earnest Christian
family of six. The parents—we will call them Patrice and William—are
intelligent and unusually resourceful people. As a couple they have
rebuilt homes together and taught themselves to farm. William now
works as a magazine editor; he has also been a college journalism
professor. Patrice is an artist. She has elected to stay at home, mainly,
until all the children are in school. So she runs the house. She also
substitute teaches, serves on the park district board, produces programs
for the local cable TV station and carves prize-winning woodcuts.

Patrice is hardly idle and unproductive. But because she draws no
salary, her neighbors assume she has nothing but empty time on her hands.
Sometimes, without asking, they drop children off at her house on their
way to work. In conversation they never inquire about how her day has
gone, for they assume that her life must be boring and "unfulfilling."

Financial pressures squeeze harder every year. William works at a demanding but not terribly well-paying job. Yet he appreciates the work, and the job allows for a life outside the office. So despite inflation and rising property taxes, Will and Patrice stick with their one-income strategy, hoping to hold out until their youngest enters kindergarten.

Other circumstances aggravate the financial pressures. The three school-age children are mocked and teased if they aren't wearing fashionable sweatshirts and running shoes. Patrice and Will struggle against the indoctrination of their children into the ways of acquisitive materialism. The battle exhausts them, since many other parents lavish money, if not time, on their children.

Our neighbors also strive to find well-crafted movies and television programs that aren't violent or sexually explicit. There aren't many. And they hear their youngest kids repeating coarse, cynical slogans they've picked up from commercials and billboards.

Sometimes I josh Will because he comes down with what I call the "cherry orchard blues." He once visited a friend who gave up a high-paying job to escape the rat race and cultivate a cherry orchard in northern Michigan. In his most beleaguered, antisuburban moods, Will talks of doing the same.

The Suckling Babe as Moral Model

Why does this couple seem so odd to their neighbors? Why are Patrice and Will so out of step with society that they fantasize about escaping to a cherry orchard? Quite simply, because they have organized their lives for the good of their children, and we live in a society that cares little for the welfare of children.

The postmodern corporation demands transient and adaptable workers. But children remain creatures that thrive only with surrounding stability. The media moguls pretend to offer frank and "mature" work.

But in fact they know their recordings, programs and films will reap few profits unless they reach the lucrative youth market. Much of their fare reeks of manipulation and disrespect for that audience. And concerned to enjoy a luxurious style of life here and now, our nation racks up debts today. Our children will have to pay for them tomorrow.

These features of our culture are signs of a deeper problem. They are manifestations of the belligerency of the bottom line, the invasion of the market into all parts of our lives. Following the logic of the economic exchange model, we have reared generations of people taught to value individualistic self-fulfillment first and foremost.

Children, of course, are naturally and unavoidably egocentric. The developmental psychologists tell us infants think the entire cosmos orbits around them. Primary in that constellation is the mother with milk. Beckoned by baby Jesselyn's cry at all hours, and thanked only by greedy, bruising lips at her breast, my wife once complained, "Sometimes I feel like nothing but a walking milk machine." Though no breast-feeder himself, Augustine thought the egocentric demands and responses of infants "are easily put up with . . . because they will disappear with increase in age."

But I want to suggest we now live in a culture that encourages us to remain childishly egocentric into and through adulthood. Breast-feeding infants excel as consumers. They focus only on their desires and their immediate gratification. In that sense the suckling babe is our premier moral model, since every institution in our society—school, church, government, entertainment media and, of course, the market—coaches us to see ourselves most fundamentally as consumers. We are remade into walking collections of felt needs looking for gratification.

But note: consumer morality "works" only as long as everyone does not try to live by it. The baby's all-dominating consumerism succeeds because Mother can imagine herself as something other than a consumer. At two in the morning she can set aside her need for sleep and go meet her child's need for nourishment. But what happens as adults increasingly lose the capacity to imagine themselves as something other than consumers? Then we can only feel more ambivalent about parenthood, because it challenges our right to remain children ourselves.

Consequently the ethic of advanced, consumeristic capitalism does not serve children well when adults try to live by it. For instance, divorce may by some measures increase the mental health and fulfillment of the former spouses; only rarely does it do the same for children. Psychologist Michael Thompson comments, "We've had a thirty-year epidemic of divorce and a generation of shell-shocked children. We have only begun to understand the long-term effects of having so many busted-up families."

Or consider a second example. Sociologist David Popenoe marshals data to argue that "more than ever before, fathers are denying paternity, avoiding their parental obligations, and [are] absent from home." As these and a dozen other examples could show, we are "disinvested" in our children, to the point that some experts have begun to refer to a national "parent deficit."

We have been coached so long and so thoroughly in the ways of autonomy and self-interest that we can no longer imagine why we should have children. After all, children cost a lot of money. And what could hinder my autonomy more than responsibility for children, who will surely impose their own expectations and limitations on my life? The only sure thing about children is that they will present their own agendas—agendas I would not have concocted for myself.

Writer Michael Dorris has wisely observed, "When you decide to have a child, you are hostage to an uncertain future." And he should know. After he adopted his son Adam, Dorris discovered the boy had Fetal Alcohol Syndrome. Determining exactly what ailed Adam, finding teachers who could educate the mentally retarded boy, helping a sometimes difficult young man find (and hold) jobs—these and dozens of other responsibilities required time, energy, patience and endurance beyond anything Dorris could have anticipated when he walked out of the adoption agency with an adorable infant in his arms.

Yet, even if to a lesser degree, isn't the same true for parents of "normal" children? If I think first and foremost of controlling my life and assuring my self-fulfillment, children make little sense. Thus even as having children regains popularity with the baby boomer generation, it doesn't fit well with our serial polygamy, our material acquisitiveness, our spite of limitations and our all-demanding career tracks. In our society, having children seems unnatural and lacks clear purpose.

Once again, then, the church finds itself in a situation that is awkward, but hopeful exactly because it is awkward. If Christians believe in bearing children—and we do—we will not find meaning, purpose and support in this task from our confused surrounding culture. Bereft of society's prop, the church is serendipitously forced back to its own story to clarify and energize the costly endeavor of Christian parenting.

Hebrews and Other Border-Crossers

In setting forth Christian interpretations of singleness and fidelity, I have tried to place our aims in terms appropriate to postmodernity. The same holds true for having children. Postmodernist writers have noted that in a world shrunken by speed and filled with rapid change, we are more than ever aware of differences. My late grandfathers, for instance, never talked to a Jew or knew an African-American on a first-name basis. Coming to maturity in postmodernity, I have studied under a Jewish professor and lived next door to an African-American couple. The postmodern world is a world where we are much more aware of and must learn to live with the "other," with those unlike us no less than those like us. In postmodern terms, then, we might say *Christians have children so we can become the kind of people who welcome strangers.*

The Christian story cares about strangers from the start. Remember that the earliest Hebrews were a ragtag collection of slaves, not all gathered from the same ethnic pool. Like strangers, they were "estranged," people without a true home and identity. The book of Exodus tells us that the Egyptian empire feared the Hebrews because their number swelled to the point that they could ally with Egyptian enemies and "escape from the land" (1:10). The powerful Egyptians, in other words, were afraid the Hebrews would cross Pharaoh's borders. Empires want above all else to control their borders. And so empires are uncomfortable with strangers, since strangers are people who are not at home. They readily cross borders. In this sense the Hebrews are the ultimate strangers, the supreme border-crossers.

Significantly, the real action in Exodus begins when the Israelites ask permission to go into the wilderness and worship. They would be gone only three days, but going into the wilderness means they will cross the border—and Pharaoh will have no border-crossing. Instead, he cruelly increases the Israelites' workload (Ex 5). In this context Walter Brueggemann observes that the term *Hebrew* apparently comes from a verb meaning "cross over." So, Brueggemann writes, "the Hebrew is one who crosses over boundaries, who has no respect for imperial boundaries, is not confined to such boundaries. . . . We can conclude that the people who finally become the 'people of God' in the Old Testament are some among those whom the empire had declared 'strangers,' 'outsiders,' 'threat.' "

The Old Testament makes it clear that the Israelites, having been outsiders themselves, were remarkably concerned about strangers. After the Hebrews became a people and looked back on the strands of their history, they remembered the story of Abraham welcoming three strangers at Mamre, and so receiving the blessing of an heir for him and Sarah (Gen 18:1-15). And after the exodus, after their own experience of being strangers in empire and wanderers in the wilderness, the Israelites had a special heart for strangers:

When an alien resides with you in your land, you shall not oppress the alien. The alien who resides with you shall be to you as the citizen among you; you shall love the alien as yourself, for you were aliens in the land of Egypt. (Lev 19:33-34)

You shall not oppress a resident alien; you know the heart of an alien, for you were aliens in the land of Egypt. (Ex 23:9)

For the LORD your God . . . loves the strangers, providing them food and clothing. You shall also love the stranger, for you were strangers in the land of Egypt. (Deut 10:17-19)

It is this story that Jesus called his own. And it propelled him into the lives of strangers, as a stranger himself. Strangers are people who cross not only geographical borders but also racial, sexual, political, moral and religious lines. Jesus spoke parables honoring such despised ethnic groups as the Samaritans, thereby ignoring racial boundaries. He scandalously taught women and conversed with them in public, thereby trespassing sexual borders. He included among his disciples Simon the Zealot and spoke the words of new life to Nicodemus the Pharisee, thereby opening himself to the array of people who were strangers to one another by virtue of their politics. He called the adulteress from the estrangement of the stoning circle back into the circle of community, thereby crossing moral borders. And he invited the ritually "unclean" to his table, thereby breaking religious taboos.

Jesus not only understood and appreciated strangers. True to his Israelite heritage, he saw himself as a stranger, a man without a home or a place to "lay his head" (Mt 8:20). Those who have learned to love the stranger know that hospitality is not simply a nicety, but "one of the pillars of morality upon which the universe stands." So a hallmark of Jesus' life and work was hospitality—even hospitality to a fault in the eyes of detractors who did not care to see him celebrating with tax collectors and sinners. Yet only by persistent attention to food, drink and hospitality could Jesus reveal the God he called Father, a generous Creator-host who gives more than we need or desire (Mt 5:43-48), a Redeemer-host who plans to greet renewed heaven and earth with a lavish wedding feast.

Meeting this God through the story of Israel and Jesus, the early church put hospitality at the center of its life. "Private" homes were opened to the Christian community (Acts 2:46; 1 Cor 16:15). These homes extended shelter and sustenance to a wide network of Christians, including missionaries and those on business trips (2 Cor 8:23). The church's central sacrament, the Eucharist, symbolizes a basic domestic activity—and that is no accident. Biological family recognizes the joyful need to solidify its union with common meals, and Paul expects the same for the church when it eats at Eucharist (1 Cor 11:17-34). Christians are called to be hospitable within both the first family of the church and the second, or biological, family, and Paul effusively praises families whose homes are the hub of the church in several cities (Rom 16:5, 23; 1 Cor 16:15, 19; Col 4:15; Philem 2).

Children as Strangers

All this may establish the importance of strangers in a Christian way of life. But what has that got to do with our own children? After all, my child lives behind my doors. I have known her from her first moments and even given her a name. There is not an hour of the day or night in which I have not held her in my arms. I have changed her diapers, wiped her nose, cleaned up her vomit. Every day I play her games, read her books, endure her temper tantrums, catalog her charms. How can she be a stranger? In terms of common sense, that doesn't make sense.

With our culture's sentimentalized view of children and family life, we would prefer to think our children are not strange. We would prefer to think that boundless parental affection is spontaneous, that we can leave behind anything like Freud's dark and steamy world of stifled desires and domestic dread. We assume that biology dictates affection and tenderness for children.

But that is simply not the case. There is no such thing as the maternal or paternal instinct, guaranteeing the safety and nurture of our children. In surveying history, an eminent historian of the family writes:

One learns about the way the writers of antiquity treated infanticide as a normal and sensible way to dispose of unwanted children; of how they amused themselves by using little children for fellatio or anal intercourse; of how the bones of child sacrifices are to be found in the foundations of buildings ranging from 7000 B.C. to 1843 A.D.; of how seventeenth-century nurses played catch-ball with the tightly swaddled infants and sometimes dropped them, with lethal consequences; of how infants were dipped in ice-cold baths, in order to harden them, or perhaps merely to baptize them, but in practice sometimes killing them; about how the doorsteps and dunghills of eighteenth-century European towns were littered with bodies of infants, dead, dying, or just abandoned; how some wet-nurses systematically starved their charges to death to save money or simply because they had accepted too many babies for their milk supply; of how children were ferociously beaten, shut up in the dark, deprived of food, terrified by bogey-men, taken to see hangings and corpses, sold into prostitution, blinded and otherwise mutilated to attract alms, castrated to supply testicles for magic, had their teeth ripped out for dentures, and in the nineteenth century suffered clitoridectomy, the attachment of toothed penile rings, and even nightly imprisonment in straitjackets to prevent masturbation—and so on, and so on, and so on.

Of course we may protest that such practices never represented the best of human nature and that many, at least, were rejected by the parents of child victims. Yet as this historian, Lawrence Stone, writes, "The cruel truth . . . may be that most parents in history have not been much involved with their children, and have not cared much about them." Stone cites anthropologists and other historians who believe even the maternal "instinct" is not universal and truly an instinct: mothers do not *necessarily* love their children.

Nor can we escape history into enlightened modern times and find that today's children are automatically friends, never strangers. For all our scientific understanding, for all our child psychology, children—even modern children—remain mysterious. We can view them via ultrasound, determine their sex and name them before they are born. We can study manuals and read the endless stream of pop psychology books that predict children's characteristics by birth order, how many siblings they have, the dysfunctions of their grandparents and so forth. But each child turns out unique. Each child loves particular games and certain sorts of songs, has a taste for broccoli or cauliflower, is frightened by this animal or that—all according to an intricate weave, here of mother's traits, here of father's attitudes, here of both parents' habits and finally of the child's own incomprehensible and original predilections. And every child, from the first midnight it bawls for a feeding to the first bizarre teenage hairstyle, often acts in ways that surprise and even distress parents. Who do not sometimes, in even the happiest of families, feel their children as intruders into their lives? Of course we know our children intimately. But we also know them as strangers.

One evidence that we find our children strange is the enduring popularity of self-help books about children. Some manuals categorize them and predict their futures. Others advise us about childrearing techniques that will form and shape the kind of person we want our child to be. If any of them "worked" as effectively as they are all touted to work, there wouldn't be so many on the market. So why do we continue to buy such books? I think this vast literature reassures us in the face of the strangeness, the alien qualities, of our children. These books say we *can* interpret and understand our children; their wildness *can* be tamed.

A more colorful evidence that we experience our children as strangers comes in the nursery rhymes and fairy tales we recite to them. "Rockabye Baby," quite apart from its tranquilizing cadence, expects dear baby and cozy cradle to be blasted out of a treetop. Perhaps it reflects the anger parents can feel even at their manifestly adorable and helpless newborn. (I remember, after rocking tiny Jesselyn through four straight hours of crying, the powerful urge to throw her through the window.)

And in seeing our children as strangers, we should not forget adult fairy tales, popular science fiction and horror stories. H. G. Wells's "The Magic Shop," Doris Lessing's *The Fifth Child,* William Peter Blatty's *The Exorcist,* Stephen King's *Children of the Corn*—all these are tales of children dangerous to adults, children possessing uncanny powers and often themselves possessed by occult or alien powers. In the old movie *Village of the Damned,* for example, the residents of a remote English town gradually and chillingly come to realize the real cause of their children's odd behavior. The children are being controlled by beings from another planet. Such fictions resonate not because we believe our children literally have supernatural powers or are likely to kill us, but because we do experience their wills and their ways as alien to our own. Think how often, upon witnessing a new behavior, parents exclaim, "Where did that come from?" or "Where did she get that?" These children may be born of our loins, but rearing them after our customs, to fit into our world, is an arduous task—one often and at least temporarily doomed to failure.

Four Ways Our Children Are Strangers

This suggests one of the ways our children are strangers to us. *They come to us as aliens and have to learn to live in our world.* Jesselyn started hating her bath at around age two. She had adored the water, kicking and splashing, even rolling full circle like a seal. Now she kicked, screamed and wriggled *before* every dip, and not in glee. Sandy and I were baffled. Then one night I noticed that Jesselyn got especially anxious toward the end of her bath, when the drain was opened. And I remembered reading that children around her age sometimes fear getting washed down the drain. They are beginning to develop a separate sense of self, but in these early days it is fragile and uncertain. At the same time they haven't learned a clear sense of proportion. So—the water disappears down the drain; what's to say their delicate, only partly formed selves won't as well?

Children can find even the most ordinary aspects of our world strange and unaccountable. For me a bath is routine. But for Jesselyn it was as exotic and suspenseful as setting off down a river that ends in a thunderous waterfall, plunging into who knows where or what.

Developmental psychologists help us understand just how different the child's world is. They remind us, for instance, that preverbal children think "magically." Objects—from teddy bears to Mother—have no independent existence. They exist only as parts of a world the child wholly controls. Baby wants them, cries for them and gets them. Wishing makes it so more often than not. So the child dwells in a world where magic works.

But parents know magic can only work for a while. We want our children to grow up and begin taking care of themselves. As they move out of infancy, we resist and even thwart more and more of their crying demands. We shatter the power of their spells and expect them to renounce their native magic. In this we are like missionaries entering a distant culture and recommending a new way of life. The toddler, psychologist Selma Fraiberg writes, is a "joyful savage" inhabiting an island paradise. But before long parents get more concerned about enculturation. At that point "the missionaries have arrived. They come bearing culture to the joyful savage. They smuggled themselves in as infatuated parents, of course. They nurtured him, made themselves indispensable to him, lured him into discovery of their fascinating world, and after a decent interval they come forth with salesmen's smiles to promote higher civilization."

The parent-missionaries promote the convenience of the cup over the breast or bottle. They prohibit simple pleasures such as sucking rocks or dried apple cores. They insist on new ways to conduct even the most intimate affairs, deriding the diaper and extolling the potty chair. "Now, admittedly, such interference is necessary in order to bring culture to a fellow who obviously needs it. But from the baby's point of view most of this culture stuff makes no sense at all. He only knows that certain vital interests are being interfered with, and since his missionaries and he do not even speak the same language, the confusion will not be cleared up for some time."

Actually, as any parent of teenagers knows, the confusion will not be cleared up for a long time indeed. Our children inhabit a different generation, have different measures of their worth, speak indecipherable and constantly shifting second languages, listen to unique music, watch bizarre movies and follow novel fashions in dress. We love them and worry over them and, happily, sometimes understand them. But they are border-crossers, resident aliens behind our doors.

Our children are also strangers to us because we are strangers to ourselves. We put little Jesselyn on the telephone to talk to her grandparents. She stands to talk, leans against the wall and crosses her ankles. "What an odd stance," I say to Sandy. "Where did she get that?" That, Sandy tells me, is how I often talk on the phone.

We are at dinner. Jesselyn drinks, and after each swallow she releases a sigh and an "ah." Before long, and with her exaggerated repetitions, I am getting irritated. "Where did she get that?" I complain. That, Sandy tells me, is something I do when I drink.

We are often too close to ourselves to see ourselves. But our children will mirror us. They will claim parts of ourselves we haven't noticed and show them back to us. Sometimes they even claim and manifest parts of ourselves we have disclaimed—such as our fear or anger.

And they vividly remind us we are creatures of culture. We are so immersed in our own culture that we forget that it, like cultures foreign to us, is odd, exotic, hard to decipher. Our children remind us. They are border-crossers with sometimes painful questions. Why do we eat animals? If Christians are supposed to love one another, how can they kill each other for their nation's sake? Why is God letting my little brother die of cancer? Can't we do anything for that homeless man?

Until we indoctrinate them, children—like border-crossers in general—see and name things about our way of life that we prefer not to see or name.

Children, and indeed all people, are strangers to us in another way. *They exist in relation to God and not simply ourselves.* We talk about "our own children," about our children "belonging" to us. That may be harmless enough, but surely it is wise to recognize that this language can mislead us. As Christians we do not and cannot own anyone—not even ourselves. Each person, a child included, is a creation of God and ultimately belongs to God. So for us there are no one-to-one relationships. There are only one-through-One relationships.

It may work a bit like the courting process. A woman spends the weekend with future in-laws. Several times her fiancé's father engages her in conversation. After the first few conversations she notices how tactfully he puts her at ease and moves questions about himself back to his deeper interest in her. After the weekend she realizes that her fiancé is also a marvelous listener. And she knows where he has picked up this skill. She has seen him more completely through his father.

We know those we know best by knowing other important people in their lives. So we can only really know other people, including our children, through the most important "person" in their lives: God. Yet we are finite creatures who can know the infinite God only partially, mysteriously. "My thoughts are not your thoughts, nor are your ways my ways," Isaiah hears God say (55:8). Since our children are first and foremost creatures of God, they will always possess possibilities we do not expect or fully understand. Though in many ways like us, they exist in relation to a God whose ways are not our ways, and who will work in their lives. They can surprise us because God can surprise us. They can cross borders because God has no borders.

Finally, children are strangers to us in a very culturally specific detail. *In a culture afraid to admit dependence, children unashamedly confess their need for others.* Children are strange to North American adults because a key characteristic of maturity, as we understand it, is independence. Yet children freely admit their dependence, recognizing they cannot survive without the generosity of others. Jesus praised this, not some innate innocence, when he advised the disciples, "Unless you change and become like children, you will never enter the kingdom of heaven" (Mt 18:3).

In this sense children cross some of our most sensitive borders. We quite carefully erect and guard personal boundaries, believing that if we achieve these we can succeed on our own. Then the whims and misfortunes of others can't threaten us. We are safe because we stand alone, in control of our destiny. But children make no such pretensions. In their bold dependence they remind us that we (and our destiny) are connected to others.

The Supreme Stranger

Christian parenthood, then, is practice in hospitality, in the welcoming and support of strangers. Welcoming the strangers who are our children, we learn a little about being out of control, about the possibility of surprise (and so of hope), about how strange we ourselves are. Moment by mundane moment—dealing with rebellion, hosting birthday parties, struggling to understand exactly what a toddler has dreamed and been so frightened by in the night—we pick up skills in patience, empathy, generosity, forgiveness. And all these are transferable skills, skills we can and must use to welcome other strangers besides our children. We become better equipped to open ourselves to strangers, especially to those strangers who are not our children but our brothers and sisters in Christ.

Yet finally, and most importantly, gaining courage to meet and love our children as strangers gives us courage to welcome the strangest stranger of them all—the God who meets us in Israel and Jesus Christ. We too easily forget just how alien and unrecognizable the God of the Bible can be, even to those who love that God. Think how Israel struggles to tell Yahweh apart from Ba'al. Think how Jesus, after his resurrection, is only gradually recognized in the garden and on the road to Emmaus. Jesus, in truth, is the supreme stranger reaching across the abyss of ultimate difference—that between the Creator and the Creator's estranged creatures. Given how we all too typically react to strangers, is it any wonder we hung the supreme stranger on a cross?

The skill, the courage our children can teach us are no small things. Our children fit us to face the true source of life without trying to kill it.

CHAPTER EIGHT

NO CHRISTIAN HOME
IS A HAVEN

●

No child can be truly secure in the hands of parents
whose care for him or her is purchased by the
neglect of other people's children. . . .

The only home which is safe for anyone to be born into
is the home that is ready to welcome someone
who does not belong there by right of kinship, but
belongs there in virtue of hospitality.
James T. Burtchaell, *For Better, for Worse*

In the night, Jesselyn runs a fever. We kiss her hot brow and administer medicine, and Sandy goes to bed with her.

I wake just before dawn, realize I am alone in the bed. So on the way to the bathroom I pause outside Jesselyn's door. My wife and my daughter sleep serenely, but the scene is one of peace after a battle. Jesselyn has feverishly tossed and turned, kicking the sheets off her and half off her mother. She lies at a 45-degree angle across the bed, one hand thrown back, palm open and resting on Sandy's hip. The baby's chapped lips are open slightly, and she breathes regularly, deeply. Sandy lies on her side, facing the doorway.

What is it about a sleeping woman and child? They move me, nearly stun me. This is the picture of innocence, of vulnerability, of complete trust, of beauty unpostured and without pretensions. What can I feel but gratitude, for this woman, this child, this moment?

Then, suddenly, bright light flashes outside Jesselyn's window. Something booms, rattling the window. Later we will find out that an electrical transformer blew just down the street. But at this fraction of a second—one of those seconds that seem much longer than a second—I wonder if the holocaust has come. Yes, it is still the time of cold war, and my imagination is saturated with cinematic and novelistic images of what happens when the nuclear bomb drops. I almost expect the walls to fall like cardboard in a gale. I can hear the whoosh, feel the heat, as a hurricane of fire surges into the bedroom. I seize one last look at the beauty and love before me, and then—

And then everything is fine. Sandy stirs, Jesselyn's hand slides from her hip, but after this they return to quiet. "It" has not happened. Today is just another day, to be started with nothing more extraordinary than a shower.

The Wall Falls

My experience was not unusual. I have talked to any number of people who saw a flash on the horizon, heard a distant explosion, started in fright when air raid sirens went off accidentally, and wondered—for a few startling seconds or minutes—if the moment of holocaust had arrived. They wondered if this was the end of their world, of family and trees and songs and promises.

At such times we realize that in our world the public and the private cannot be so easily and neatly separated as we have imagined. The dark possibility of nuclear holocaust cannot be confined to the public world of politics and war. For politics and war can destroy the private world of family and friendship. The shadow of the holocaust dims and overcomes the false, bright line we good moderns and capitalists draw between our public lives and our private lives.

Other realities of our complicated societies make the split between public and private less plausible, less practical in our day and age. Ecological concerns such as the greenhouse effect and the deterioration of the ozone layer mean that the environmental irresponsibility of public corporations across the country—indeed, across the continents—can make our private neighborhoods unlivable.

Economically, as we have seen, it is no less difficult to draw a clear line between the public and the private. The belligerence of the bottom line means we shape our private lives according to the economic exchange model. We attempt to construct families like businesses, to conduct the ministry of the church like a marketing strategy. Also, the economic fortunes of private households in America rise and fall according to what happens with crop-destroying droughts in the Ukraine, grabs for oil and power in the Persian Gulf, struggles for governmental supremacy in Afghanistan and Vietnam. We wake up, hear the morning news and find the most intimate corners of our lives invaded and changed by events in a country that, the day before, we could not have found on a map.

And the morning news, of course, is representative of the public media that pervade our supposedly private lives. We watch the quite public phenomenon of television in the sanctity of our homes, listen to the radio alone in our cars. Technology and media have shrunk the world, brought the public and real world back into our living rooms.

In more ways than one, our postmodern situation is paradoxical. As sociologist Alan Wolfe has observed, just when we seem to have forgotten how to preserve small families, we must strengthen massive societies and globe-spanning economies. We live in a time when we need one another more and trust one another less. In societies where we must care for strangers, we don't know how to treat our loved ones.

Postmodernity breaks down the modern wall between the public and the private. Unfortunately, Christians often resist the demolition of this wall, loudly insisting, for example, that the home must remain a (private) haven. We need to see that the fall of modernity's wall—a collapse more significant than that of the Berlin Wall—presents Christian family with new challenges and fresh opportunities.

Secularization and Divided Lives

Our modern culture, fixated on such values as autonomy and efficiency, has thrived on the separation of the public and the private. We are most autonomous and efficient when messy human relationships, with all the imaginative and emotional involvement that comes with them, can be pushed aside. We are the best capitalists and consumers when we can perform in an economy that operates as if people don't matter, or at least don't need to be seen as people but as "human resources." At its extreme, the strict separation of public and private creates such lives as that of John D. Rockefeller, the notorious oil "robber baron" in public life and devout Baptist in private life. Addressing a Sunday-school class, Rockefeller once declared:

> The growth of a large business is merely a survival of the fittest.
> . . . The American Beauty rose can be produced in the splendor and
> fragrance which bring cheer to its beholder only by sacrificing the
> early buds which grow up around it. This is not an evil tendency in
> business. It is merely the working-out of a law of nature and a law
> of God.

At home, in the bosom of the family—love, generosity, humanity. But at work, survival of the fittest as a law of nature and (an unbiblical and impersonal) God. Rockefeller never understood that his faith might have something to do with his business practices. What we are talking about in divided lives such as Rockefeller's is secularization.

Secularization has been a hot topic in the Christian community for many years. But for all our concern about secularization, we have largely accepted the public-private distinction and seen secularization's main characteristic to be the erosion of the authority of formal religion in the lives of individuals.

By contrast, I see secularization's main and most insidious characteristic to be the separation of the public and the private. Under our cultural arrangement, the public is the realm of objectivity and "fact." The private is the realm of subjectivity and "value." Science, politics and economics arbitrate in the public realm; religion is relegated to the private realm. With this arrangement, all the people in the world could go to church thrice weekly and the Christian faith would have no public significance. It is merely one more private preference, or "value."

So pietistic Christians are the world's leading secularists when they emphasize that Jesus Christ is Lord "of my heart." The biblical attestation is that Christ is Lord "of my heart" *because* he is first and foremost Lord of the cosmos. The New Testament sees the church (and not the individual) as key to Christian witness because it sees Christ as a public and not merely a private Lord. The church is the communal, public body that recognizes what one day the entire world will: that Christ is ruler of all nations and all peoples.

Yet Christians remain willing to concede the separation of public and private because there is a tradeoff. Remember the account unpacked in chapter three: We will let the public world be inhuman because we are promised that the private world will be supremely human. The private world will be our haven and retreat. At home, within the family, we will be treated as persons and loved "just for who we are."

As we have seen, the public-private split is failing even on its own terms. But we Christians should especially object to an arrangement that trivializes faith and reduces Yahweh to a household god, Jesus to a domestic mascot. Quite simply, the church's story does not admire autonomy and efficiency so intensely. Rather than viewing commitment to Christ as a private preference, akin to my taste in movies or music, it sees this commitment as the pivotal and crucial truth of my entire life—no less public than private. This story requires me (and my family) to be part of a community, a social body that witnesses to the public as well as the private truth of Christ. If I am to live by this story, I must learn to see strangers as persons and not merely ciphers or functionaries. I must let down the walls between public and private, for they are not walls erected by God.

The Not-So-Private Households of Rome

I suppose the strict separation of public and private has so captured our imaginations that it stretches us to think of the home as something other than a private haven. But we can remind ourselves that through the centuries—pretty much up until the Industrial Revolution—millions of people have lived and died with another understanding of home and family. And we should certainly recall how odd such a separation would have appeared in the biblical world.

Like the Hebrew culture, Roman society made no sharp separation between public and private life. Scholars tell us that household relationships we consider private and individual carried important social and political baggage in the Roman world. Greek influences were important, of course. Plato saw marriage as the most fundamental concern of the city legislator. And the Stoic Antipater called marriage a *civic* "obligation of the first order."

No doubt the home was a place of comfort and rest for Roman family members, especially the paterfamilias, or male head. But streams of commerce and politics flowed daily through the home. There the paterfamilias paid court to clients. Clients were those he sponsored in public life, such as poets and philosophers dependent on patrons for a livelihood. So the paterfamilias's social and political obligations did not end when he crossed the threshold into his home. If anything, those obligations began there.

These facts rehearsed, we do well to remember that the early church was based in the households of Rome. The Christians of the New Testament worshiped together in their homes, welcomed and supported missionaries in homes, evangelized in homes, assisted the poor in homes and challenged the undue claims of Caesar in homes. On all counts, they regarded the home as something more significant, more challenging, more exciting than a haven.

The Christian Home Is a Mission Base

Now of course I am not suggesting that we attempt the wholesale transplantation of the Hebrew or New Testament style of household into twentieth-century North America. I mention the biblical homes only as a reminder that the isolated, privatized nuclear family is not—like the earth spinning round the sun or rain falling when a cloud bursts—the result of natural law. Nor is our privatized nuclear family *the* biblical model. In fact, there is nothing like this family in the Old or the New Testament.

Thus the family structures and customs found in the Bible, so unlike our own, force us to be creatively faithful. They will not allow us to anoint the nineteenth-century bourgeois family by casually reading it into the biblical text. They do not offer universal formulas about how to practice Christian family. They push us to search for and be true to the underlying theological truths, truths about who God is and what God hopes for creation, truths revealed in the story of Israel and Jesus. They demand that we live with God and one another for our own day, that we break down the wall dividing the public and the private in our own way. Three theological truths challenge that wall.

1. God is creator of all that is. The God revealed through Israel and Jesus does not create merely the individual or "spiritual" parts of our world. He has created the political realm as well as the psychological realm, the marketplace as well as the bedroom.

2. Jesus is Lord of all. The redeemer and liberator of the world died and rose for all aspects of creation. His lordship extends beyond the private, inward and mystical to the public, outward and political.

3. Through Israel and Jesus, God has demonstrated care for the stranger. God reaches out to those who are forgotten or oppressed, who are homeless and lost. God's people are expected to do the same.

Put in terms relevant to our postmodern world, *we need to break down the wall between the public and the private in order to let God be God of our entire lives.* The effects of secularization have shown us that if God is not God of all parts of our lives, God is not really God of any part of our lives. The household god admired by industrialization and capitalism is not the Yahweh of Israel. The privatized Jesus is not the Jesus who, at the cross, "disarmed the rulers and authorities and made a public example of them, triumphing over them" (Col 2:15).

All this has some quite practical—and profound—consequences. A key consequence is that no Christian home is a haven. Christians in our society must retrain themselves to see faith as no less public than private. To be true to our story, we cannot imagine that anyone's public and personal lives are finally separable. We must be "just who we are" (that is, persons whose identities are based in and on Christ) in public no less than in private. In a real sense, and like the homes of the New Testament church, our homes must go public. Our call is to live not in private havens or retreats, but in mission bases.

Key to this, of course, is hospitality—to our children, to other

Christians and to the stranger who comes with another faith or no faith at all. Though by no means shutting out the world, the New Testament emphasizes hospitality to others within the church. Such hospitality is not just a private act or way of being. With food and drink, with the sharing of possessions and time, with the generous opening of our lives, we sustain and celebrate one another as the free gifts of God. As Paul had it, we show—no, we *are—Christ* to the world by being his body, by worshiping together, helping one another materially and spiritually, using gifts of the Spirit for the common good (1 Cor 12). So welcoming our Christian sisters and brothers is a public act and way of being. It makes Christ publicly available and evident.

In our society, we have been prone to imagine that we can live privately and individually as Christians with or without the social support of the church. We were able to suffer this illusion because America has been nominally Christian, or at least Judeo-Christian. Many of our customs and ethics were lent social support and plausibility by the society as a whole. In effect, without entirely admitting it to ourselves, we let the society serve as our church. When we assume the problems of poverty and injustice will be solved governmentally, we expect the state to serve as the church. When we present Christian discipleship as a prudent investment, we make the market into the church. But as our culture removes more and more of its nominally Christian props, we will entertain fewer such illusions. The church itself will have to be the church.

Chaste Rebels and Other Witnesses

But what can it mean for the church to be the church, to walk through the crumbling public-private dividing wall? Once again, I fear our imagination has been maimed and constricted by the enthusiastic Christian adoption of the public-private split. So let me here offer three quite concrete examples of how that split can be mended.

1. Sex. The Christian way of life calls for sex to be practiced and enjoyed within marriage. So we call our children to wait. Yet as philosopher Alasdair MacIntyre writes, "Any conception of chastity as a virtue . . . in a world unformed by either Aristotelian or biblical values will make very little sense to the dominant culture." We now live in a world unformed by biblical (or Aristotelian) values. As I have emphasized, our society's understanding of sexual behavior now owes as much or more to the economic exchange model as it does to Christianity. Now the dominant culture, through its schools, popular media and medical establishment, encourages teenagers to experiment sexually.

According to its own ethic, emphasizing autonomous choice and admiring pleasure as one of the highest goods, the economic exchange culture is acting responsibly when it helps teenagers safely explore and "find themselves" sexually. Chastity is weird and unhealthy in this context. The chaste person unaccountably forecloses his or her choices of a mate or "sexual partner." The married person who lives in fidelity to a mate misses out on a variety of available options. All this means that in our society only rebels are chaste. To live by countercultural values and abstain from premarital sex, we and our children must be part of a community that makes chastity credible and admirable.

Thus sex, supposedly a supremely private matter, is a profoundly public concern. Without the support of others outside their immediate family, our children can only see chastity as implausible and unrealistic. In the area of sexuality and many others, we cannot be Christians individually without being Christians together; we cannot be Christian family without being linked to other Christian families.

2. Housing. The plight of the homeless in our cities offers one more example of how awkward it is for a postmodern world to pretend the public and private can be strictly separated. After all, the home is the epitome of the private. Yet when thousands of our fellow citizens—men, women and children—lose their homes, we instinctively turn to the public realm of government for a solution.

It would be foolish to deny the importance of governmental participation in facing problems like homelessness. But Christians who think this is the only or even best response display stunted imagination. Habitat for Humanity is an example of a more robust Christian imagination at work. Habitat goes to people in need of homes, with resources *and* Christian men and women who labor beside the homeless to build a house. Thus Habitat's ministry requires its ministers to live and work with the homeless. In other words, in the name of Jesus they engage and form relationships with those to whom they would minister. New Testament scholar Richard Hays remarks, "The [biblical] texts call neither for government action *nor* private philanthropy; instead, they summon the *church* to the need of the homeless. For that reason . . . Habitat for Humanity represents an impressively faithful response to the New Testament witness: It mobilizes God's people directly to do what . . . the texts require."

3. Race. A few years ago a Presbyterian church in Madison, Wisconsin, got committed to helping kids the public school considered "at risk" of dropping out. At first, and admirably enough, the church provided tutoring. But it became apparent that these young students needed more than assistance in algebra. Many lived in poverty and broken families. They had no reason to do well in school as long as they had to go home to despair every night. In other words, they drew no clear line between the public world of schooling and the private world of their families. They could not do well at school without doing well at home.

Realizing this, the church's first impulse was to launch a crusade. It singled out all the public agencies and educational institutions that should be lobbied and manipulated to meet its goals. That is, after all, how the system works. But when some of the church folk heard themselves talking in this vein, they stopped in their tracks. As pastor Craig Barnes explains in his book *Yearning,* "We then began to ask the better questions: 'What is it that the church is uniquely qualified to do here? How has life in God's kingdom equipped us to respond to this great need in our city?' It wasn't long before we stopped acting like angry lobbyists."

Instead, the church reached out directly to the families of the students at risk. "We started working harder on relationships, and less on our naive hopes of alleviating poverty and racism for all of Madison. This made the kids and their families less of 'the problem' and more of the valuable people we wanted to love," writes Barnes. The church cooperated with a local foundation and business leaders to provide college scholarships for kids who graduated from high school. Besides building relationships with families, it provided mentors for students, eventually partnering with a black church so that black kids would have familiar role models.

In the process, Barnes's church confronted racism and learned, in his words, that "reconciling is the language of relationships, not problem-solving." For years Madison's white and black churches had talked about racism, "but never to each other," he writes. "We now have that discussion with our brothers and sisters frequently, but only because we have a relationship with them."

Barnes admits that some have worried about combining mission programs with churches of other denominations, and working so closely with public schools and civic groups. Such endeavors seem to threaten the privatized purity and serenity of the church. But in attempting to respond to needs "by the norms of the kingdom rather than the world," this church desecrated the idol of public and private separation. Those concerned for the purity of the church "cautioned us that this partnering would have the effect of making the walls around the church appear fuzzy and confusing," Barnes writes. "We hope they are right."

When a Home Is Not a Haven

All three of these examples involve the imaginative formation and activity of Christian community. They involve a recognition (quite compatible with the postmodern frame of mind) that Christianity is known not so much by what people intellectually affirm as by how they live. But even yet our imaginations may falter. The examples of sex, housing and race hint at how individual families need and work through the church. But how, exactly, is the home itself a mission base?

The Christian home is a mission base when Christians live in intentional community, such as Chicago's Jesus People U.S.A. or Washington's Sojourners Fellowship. But the Christian home is also a mission base when Christians who happen to live in the same neighborhood enjoy meals together, share a lawn mower and tree-trimming tools, or "exchange" kids for an occasional evening.

The Christian home is a mission base when we refuse to "shop" for churches after one church has bored or inconvenienced us. This tendency betrays the blatant consumerization of our faith. When a family struggles to stay with a church through bad times, it demonstrates another way of life than that so relentlessly promoted by the economic exchange model.

The Christian home is a mission base when, as in one case I know about, three families covenant that no one family will take jobs and move to another city unless all three families, through prayer and mutual consideration, decide they will go as well. Likewise, the Christian home is a mission base when members of a church move into the same apartment complex, sponsor Bible studies and organize supervision of the playground.

The Christian home is a mission base when a family opens its home. Sandy and I have enjoyed some of our richest Christian community when, on two occasions, single friends lived with us while they were marooned between apartments. Each stayed with us only for a matter of weeks, but even that was time to strengthen ties.

The point is simple. In a world that offers less and less nominal support of Christian practices, in a world increasingly fragmented, hostile and lonely, in a world that insistently attempts to atomize our lives and privatize our faith, there is no end to ways the Christian home can serve as a mission base. The limit, quite literally, is our imagination.

Intimacy Is Not Enough

I hope that through all these instances of Christian community one thing is clear. The church is not interested in community simply for the family's sake. We practice hospitality and build community because the story of Israel and Jesus calls for it. The necessity of hospitality converts our homes from insulated havens into adventurous mission bases. Hospitality gives families a purpose beyond themselves. They exist to serve God and the world through the church.

With the private-public separation and the idealization of the home as a haven, I am afraid Christian families today often live for themselves. They think the church exists to serve them. They buy books that make spiritual disciplines important *because* they will strengthen the family, that tell them to go to church *because* going to church will make the family happier. But this gets it all backwards. "The family that prays together, stays together" is not such an innocent statement. It is in fact just one more way to pervert both the church and the gospel according to the dictates of the economic exchange model. If we worship and pray to God because that will strengthen our family, then we make worship and prayer (and God) into investment techniques that serve our ends. And ironically, the family hurts itself when it makes the family the goal and object of Christian mission and spiritual disciplines.

Kingdom mission and Christian hospitality and community are not instrumental. They are not undertaken *in order to* strengthen and make families happy. The strength and happiness of families is an important thing. But it is a byproduct of service to a kingdom larger than the family, not the object of the service to that kingdom. To be healthy, the family needs a mission or purpose beyond itself.

As we have seen earlier in these pages, family in times and places past served many purposes. Children provided needed labor. Parents educated their offspring in the crafts that would be their livelihood. Arranged marriages bound adult children more tightly to the extended family. Consequently there were a variety of interdependencies between parents and children, a variety of functions holding families together.

Today this great variety of purposes and functions has been whittled away. Understanding family as a private realm, our culture has only one real function for it: intimacy. Now family has no ties to the public world. It is supposed to exist simply for itself. It is a place we can cultivate and enjoy mutual affection. This modern form of family has its advantages. I know of few things more deeply satisfying than moments of spontaneous, mutual affection with my family and friends. And perhaps these moments are more frequent than in, say, my grandparents' day—more frequent in a world that constantly coaches us to be aware of and express our feelings.

But what will make family exciting, what will make it worthy of our commitment and take us through the dry times, is common commitment to a mission bigger than our family. Christian families commit themselves to the church; the church commits itself to the kingdom. When affection wanes, spouses are still committed to witnessing God's fidelity, to rearing children who can serve the world in Christ, to providing a place hurt people can come for healing.

The long and short of it is that we simply need a world bigger, richer, tougher than that which can be created by a little family fixated on itself and its emotional coddling. We need a cause large and exciting enough that many people, not just a spouse and two or three children, can devote their lives to it. As theologian Paul Waddell writes, it is the commitment of other people to the same cause that convinces us that the work "to which we have given our life is truly worth our life." It is the various ministries and joys of many families that show us how rich and varied are the goods and gifts of the kingdom. One family sponsors a refugee, another adopts multiracial children, a third staffs a soup kitchen on Thanksgiving Day. Such an array of hospitality proves that the kingdom is expansive and bountiful indeed, that one or even one hundred families cannot exhaust its potential. It deserves my life. It deserves the life of my family.

The Mission of Celebration

Perhaps the kingdom deserves the life of my family. Perhaps my home should be a mission base rather than a haven. But it all sounds so—well, tiring. In our frenetic society, many families find both parents working and children involved in dozens of activities. We struggle to keep up.

One family left my church because its "needs weren't being met." But this was no trivial and selfish complaint. A son was on drugs. A daughter showed signs of serious rebellion. A third, and autistic, child demanded increasing attention. This family was not just looking for more warm fuzzies. Its very survival was at stake. Did it need to hear that it should become a mission base rather than a haven?

In one word, yes. And at that point of deepest desperation and pain more than ever. For what a tired, frenetic world needs to know and see as much as anything is that an integral feature of Christian mission is rest and celebration.

Of course there are times when families simply need to rest. But remember that we live in a society that esteems autonomy as one of its highest goods. In our society the individual is independent, ideally depending on no one and nothing. And individuals who depend only on themselves must always be on guard. They can never rest. Thus we live in a world that might be characterized above all else as restless.

Yet Jews and Christians are peculiar people who celebrate the sabbath rest and understand that rest as one of the most crucial aspects of our witness. Unlike others in our society, we claim that our lives do not belong to us and are not in our control. We claim there is a Creator who trusts the goodness of his creation enough even to rest himself on the seventh day! How better can we show that the world and its welfare do not depend on us and our efforts than to rest regularly and boldly? How better to show that the world is good enough to believe in than to let it be one day a week?

What's more, as scholar Richard Horsley notes, "a strikingly distinctive activity of Jesus and his followers was their regular celebration with festive meals." Jesus' frequent eating and drinking—his partying—was a celebration of the kingdom that had come, and an anticipation of the greatest of all banquets that God will host when the kingdom achieves its fullness. They who would be at home in the kingdom had better learn how to party, and Jesus apparently made sure his disciples had plenty of practice. There was so much practice, in fact, that the most pious believers of the day scorned Jesus as a "glutton and a drunkard" (Lk 7:34).

They were actually quoting Scripture at Jesus, and their choice of text was interesting. In full, Deuteronomy 21:18-21 reads:

If someone has a stubborn and rebellious son who will not obey his father and mother, who does not heed them when they discipline him, then his father and his mother shall take hold of him and bring him out to the elders of his town at the gate of that place. They shall say to the elders of his town, "This son of ours is stubborn and rebellious. He will not obey us. He is a glutton and a drunkard." Then all the men of the town shall stone him to death. So you shall purge the evil from your midst; and all Israel will hear, and be afraid.

We should remember that the words hurled at Jesus were hurled by people who knew their Bible well, and would have been aware of the context surrounding the epithet "glutton and drunkard." Perhaps, then, they regarded his unbecoming party habit as of a piece with his challenge to the supremacy of the family as they understood it. Remember that this was the man who, running hard against the current of his culture, claimed his disciples and not his blood relatives as his first family. So perhaps behind the accusation "glutton and drunkard" resonated an unspoken but implied question: "What else would you expect from a stubborn and rebellious son?"

At any event, on the counts of sabbath-keeping and Jesus' festive demeanor, to deny that the Christian home is a haven is not to deny it the necessity of rest and the joy of celebration. Instead, in the light of the sabbath and Jesus, we are called to see the family in a new way. Decentered by the church, isolated family does not offer us the prime group loyalty of our lives. Now the Christian family is a mission base in service of its larger and enclosing first family, the church. And when the Christian home is a mission base, rest and celebration are not purely private. They are among the most important features of Christian witness, and so among our most significant public acts.

Burnout: From the Rocket to the Cross

The popular concept for what so many families experience in a restless world is burnout. They are exhausted, empty, have no remaining energy to go on. The underlying imagery comes from rocket science. A rocket has only so much fuel; it ignites, shoots into the atmosphere and, once its fuel runs out, falls spent back to earth.

But notice how the rocket imagery of burnout plays on our culture's specious separation of the public and the private. In a sense, burnout creates the condition it describes and deplores. After all, rockets are solitary and self-contained. They have no resources outside themselves. Once the fuel they bear is exhausted, *they* are exhausted, never to fly again. The rocket imagery also assumes that activities can only exhaust us. Rockets cannot generate energy at the same time they expend it.

Now, if we are isolated individuals dependent on our own energy, the rocket imagery fits. But the Christian confession is that people aren't rockets. The prime imagery of Christ's kingdom—the cross—assumes that the real gifts we receive flow from our giving, that genuine energy comes from spending energy rather than hoarding it. And it assumes that bearing the cross is a community affair. Seen in the shadow of the cross rather than the rocket, then, certain activities, public as well as private, can energize and refresh us even as we exert ourselves.

I am saying that burnout is largely a matter of interpretation, of how we see and understand the situation we are in. For instance, many of us expend more physical energy at our private leisure than our public work. I use more calories in an hour of jogging than during eight hours in front of my word processor. Being physically and even mentally exhausted doesn't necessarily mean I'm burned out. In fact, I *feel* refreshed after a run.

Work can energize. Good work often does. One year I was especially frustrated with my job, feeling constricted, confused, increasingly embittered. I was burning out. For vacation, I chose to go home to

Oklahoma and help with wheat harvest. From some perspectives, this
should have assured burnout. It meant fourteen-hour days, sweat and
itchy chaff, the incessant noise of combines, trucks, grain elevators. But
by the third or fourth day of harvest I was coming alive. Hour after hour,
I watched the rows of sliced wheat straw fall neatly and dependably
before the combine's sickle. I watched the grain, like a soothing waterfall, pour into the bin behind me. I fell into sync with the pounding
rhythms of the machine. Sweating and itching, I sensed my body again.
I was diverted. My imagination roamed and found new places from
which to view my job. Eventually I recognized—and sympathized
with—concerns of my employer that I had never imagined before.
Rambling through the corridors of memory, I recalled joys of my job
that had been forgotten but were still available.

I went back to my livelihood with a sunburn, in need of some sleep,
but absolutely energized. What if I had simply said to myself, "No,
wheat harvest is *work* [which it certainly is]; you'll burn out for sure.
Work is public; vacations are for private life. Go hide in the mountains
of New Mexico"? Then I would have missed one of the most refreshing
and enjoyable vacations of my life.

We burn out because we do not recognize that public life can be
energizing as well as exhausting. We burn out because we compartmen-
talize our lives and can only loosely—and with continual effort—hold
the parts together. Each of us becomes an array of public and private
selves without any center or sense of wholeness. Who am I? One
moment I am a public editor, now a private father. One hour I am a
public grocery buyer, then I go back home to be a private husband. I am
constantly changing roles and having to redefine myself both to myself
and to those I meet. I am saying that service to the kingdom provides
the center and sense of wholeness we otherwise lack. It crosses public-
private lines and unites these supposedly separate worlds.

Christian family, of all places, is where we put our lives back together, where we live not so much in a public or private world as in God's one good and redeemed world. The Christian home is a mission base. It is where we strain and labor and sometimes weep in service to the kingdom. But it is also where we learn to "do" mission as rest and play, where welcoming friends and reading novels and planting gardens and making babies are among our noblest moral endeavors. It is where we do both our most strenuous and our most refreshing work—for what could be more strenuous and more refreshing than rearing children?

I love Jesselyn so intensely and with so much energy that I sometimes worry that a second child would surely be slighted. I said as much to a friend who had seen her second child and beyond. "I used to think the same thing myself," she said. "But the second just creates more love to go around." It must be a related logic and power that causes God to draw more and more people into the kingdom, to the feast that awaits.

Acknowledgments & Notes

While polishing the final draft of this book, I have listened to Wynton Marsalis's exquisite *Thick in the South* and been reminded of my envy of musicians who, in a "tight" set, create something special together. By contrast, writing seems a solitary craft, requiring long hours of isolation in the library or at the computer keyboard. And yet writing may not be so different from jazz. Like jazz, writing demands both discipline and spontaneity. And the writer, like the jazz soloist, is never really alone or original, but can at best improvise on themes already generously provided. How rich and wonderful, then, is the tradition and community enabling me to attempt my own "jazz," inadequate as it may be.

In a book about family, it seems appropriate to break with custom and thank my family first rather than last. This book is dedicated to my father. Among his many gifts to me was that he taught me how to persevere with work even when I disliked it. Writing is often arduous, unrewarding for days and weeks at a time. But because Dad made me bale and stack hay, I am now capable of finishing a book.

My happy debt to my wife, Sandy, may be as great. She is my companion in the fullest possible sense of the word. Really, I've grown up with her. Though we are only in our mid-thirties, we've been married fifteen years and some say we're beginning to look alike. That is surely to my advantage. As for daughter Jesselyn, the variety of nicknames she's inspired (Burl, the boxcar girl, Jezzbo, Jester, Boster, the tiny barbarian and so forth) suggest how she stirs the imagination.

As for debts outside my second family (but still within first family), I began to seriously reflect on the topic when I read Stanley Hauerwas's *A Community of Character* in 1985. Stanley's radical Christian vision, appreciation of narrative and liturgy, and dedication of his craft to the church have stimulated me as I have read and reread his work in the years since. He generously increased my debt by providing bibliographic leads, and by closely reading and commenting on this book's penultimate draft. Another important scholarly mentor has been Lauree Hersch Meyer, who shepherded me through the first and second drafts, tutored me in Augustine and H. Richard Niebuhr, and taught me how to think analogically.

Finally, I'm delighted to thank a number of other friends and colleagues. With his usual (yea, near legendary) skill and grace, James Hoover edited this book. The folk at St. Barnabas Episcopal Church heard and sharpened my ideas at an early stage. I was encouraged by members of LaSalle Street Church who, on a fall retreat, heard these ideas at a late stage. A host of other friends offered discernment after reading all or part of the book in one draft or another, or passed articles or books on to me. They include Bob Bittner, Micah Blalock, Michael Cameron, Jeffry Davis, Lorraine Davis, Phillip Ellsworth, Douglas Frank, Craig Keener, Mickey Maudlin, Greg Metzger, David Neff, Don Richter, Robin Sheffield, Kathryn Siska, Don Stephenson, Lynda Rutledge Stephenson, Mary Stewart Van Leeuwen and Douglas Webster. To one and all, my deepest and ongoing gratitude.

CHAPTER 1: Postmodernity

James Davison Hunter is quoted from *Evangelicalism: The Coming Genera-*

tion (Chicago: University of Chicago Press, 1987), p. 76. Tim LaHaye's book is *The Battle for the Family* (Old Tappan, N.J.: Revell, 1982). James Dobson and Gary Bauer's book is *Children at Risk: The Battle for the Hearts and Minds of Our Kids* (Dallas: Word Books, 1990). And Pat Robertson's volume is *The New Millennium* (Dallas: Word Books, 1990). On Jack Kemp's presidential campaigning, see Randall Balmer, *Mine Eyes Have Seen the Glory: A Journey into the Evangelical Subculture in America* (New York: Oxford University Press, 1989), p. 118. For James Robison's theology of family and nation, consult his *Attack on the Family* (Wheaton, Ill.: Tyndale House, 1980), p. 7. For a brief history of the evangelical response to capitalism throughout the twentieth century, see Craig M. Gay, "When Evangelicals Take Capitalism Seriously," *Christian Scholar's Review* 21 (June 1992): 343-61. I quote Robert Nisbet from *The Present Age* (New York: Harper & Row, 1988), p. 118.

The Amish Reminder

The church is called the "last great stronghold of family idolatry" by Mary Jo Weaver in her "Single Blessedness," *Commonweal*, October 26, 1979, pp. 588-91. Weaver writes of the Roman Catholic Church, but I suspect her criticism may be even more true of the Protestant evangelical church.

On the Puritan family, see Steven Mintz and Susan Kellogg, *Domestic Revolutions: A Social History of American Family Life* (New York: Free Press, 1988), pp. 1-23, particularly p. 15; and Philip J. Lee, *Against the Protestant Gnostics* (New York: Oxford University Press, 1987), pp. 118-19 and 136-37.

I write in this section that Christians in each generation are called to read the biblical story anew and, without trying to mimic the pioneers of our faith, respond to the story within the particular challenges and privileges of our culture. Readers who are curious about what such a reading strategy would mean in detail may want to consult the wonderfully lucid (and amazingly brief) book of Stephen E. Fowl and L. Gregory Jones, *Reading in Communion: Scripture and Ethics in Christian Life* (Grand Rapids, Mich.: Eerdmans, 1991). I have in mind roughly the same approach Ched Myers calls a "socio-literary reading strategy." The introductory and methodological section of his *Binding the Strong Man: A Political Reading of Mark's Story of Jesus* (Maryknoll, N.Y.: Orbis Books, 1988), pp. 3-87, lays this out quite nicely. (Unfortunately, portions of Myers's reading of the Gospel itself are reductionistic—seeing, for instance, *only* Palestinian politics where Mark's Gospel sees transcendent demonic powers at work.)

I hint that it is philosophers such as Kant who have taught us we did not need to rely on particular religious traditions and specific historical communities to know the truth. It is along these lines that we have been misleadingly convinced there is such a category as "religions" and Christianity is but one specimen among them. Consequently, much interreligious dialogue is undertaken with the belief in a kind of "pluralism" that assumes all religions are at bottom alike. Kenneth Surin observes, "A major practical problem is . . . created, because this pluralism decrees, in advance and a priori as it were, that *anything* which the Hindu and the Christian bring to this dialogue . . . has an equivalence that is imposed, by the mechanisms of this subtending pluralism, independently of their socially and culturally governed languages and forms of life. In [John] Hick's scheme, for instance, all phenomenal inequalities and non-equivalences are effectively overridden by the noumenal unavailability of the Real." Hick, in short, relies on Kantian categories (the phenomenal and the noumenal) to say how all religions are alike. Ironically, the pluralism of Christian theologian John Hick would not wish that all people become Christians, but it requires that we all (Christian and Hindu alike) be Kantians! Such is the danger of the false universalism of post-Enlightenment thought. See

Surin, "A 'Politics of Speech,' " in *Christian Uniqueness Reconsid-
ered: The Myth of a Pluralistic Theology of Religions,* ed. Gavin
D'Costa (Maryknoll, N.Y.: Orbis Books, 1990), pp. 192-212 (quote
from p. 204). From the same volume, and along similar lines, see John
Milbank, "The End of Dialogue," pp. 174-91. Also in this volume, and
in his characteristically clear fashion, John B. Cobb Jr. critiques the
post-Enlightenment rubric of "religions" ("Beyond 'Pluralism,' " pp.
81-95).

The Stumbling Giant
On speed and the shrinking of the world, see David Harvey, *The Condition
of Postmodernity* (London: Basil Blackwell, 1989), p. 241. Charles Taylor
is quoted from his *Sources of the Self* (Cambridge, Mass.: Harvard University
Press, 1989), p. 313.

Another Name for Nowhere
Jeffrey Stout, in *The Flight from Authority* (Notre Dame, Ind.: University of
Notre Dame Press, 1981), offers an excellent account of how religious
turmoil caused early moderns to turn to reason and away from traditional
authority for their guiding star. The relegation of religion to private life is an
important theme to be unpacked throughout the present book. In anticipation
of this and other themes relevant to our present purposes, it is worth noting
the candor and clarity of conservative columnist George F. Will, who writes
that America's founders "wished to tame and domesticate religious passions
of the sort that convulsed Europe. They aimed to do so not by establishing
religion, but by establishing a commercial republic—capitalism. They aimed
to submerge people's turbulent energies in self-interested pursuit of material
comforts." Will goes on to say, "Religion is to be perfectly free as long as it
is perfectly private." This is exactly the sort of freedom I will argue the church
cannot afford if it is going to remain faithful to the gospel. Will is quoted in

Stanley Hauerwas, *After Christendom?* (Nashville: Abingdon, 1991), p. 30.

On how evolution has been interpreted and employed, see Bram Dijkstra, *Idols of Perversity* (New York: Oxford University Press, 1986), p. 160; and Richard Hofstadter, *Social Darwinism in American Thought* (New York: George Braziller, 1959), pp. 161-67, and, for the quote from Darwin, p. 179. That Darwin's science was inseparable from his time and place has recently been confirmed by the authoritative biography *Darwin,* by Adrian Desmond and James Moore (New York: Warner Books, 1992). As they write, " 'Social Darwinism' is often taken to be something extraneous [to Darwin's science], an ugly concretion added to the pure Darwinian corpus after the event, tarnishing Darwin's image. But his notebooks make plain that competition, free trade, imperialism, racial extermination, and sexual inequality were written into the equation from the start—'Darwinism' was always intended to explain human society." Reviewing this book, historian Mark A. Noll observes that "Desmond and Moore show that theoretical science has never been a neutral, objective, detached exercise." For Noll, they "reinforce the conclusion that one of the most persistent, and most pernicious, delusions of our time is that scientific data—especially on questions of human origin—can speak for themselves." Instead, as he quite correctly and elegantly concludes, "Facts, however assiduously collected, never explain themselves. Overarching explanations of facts always coexist with economic interests, political aspirations, religious sympathies and competition for personal standing." See "Theology, Science, Politics: What Darwin Meant," *The Christian Century,* August 26—September 2, 1992, pp. 776-79 (the quote from Desmond and Moore is drawn from this review).

On the cultural specificity of science and reason itself, see, for an accessible introduction, William Placher, *Unapologetic Theology* (Louisville, Ky.: Westminster/John Knox, 1989). My own understanding owes much to Alasdair MacIntyre, *After Virtue,* 2nd ed. (Notre Dame, Ind.: University of Notre Dame Press, 1984), and *Whose Justice? Which Rationality?* (Notre Dame, Ind.: University of Notre Dame Press, 1988). A breathtakingly bold postmodern theological reinterpretation of our situation is John Milbank, *Theology and Social Theory: Beyond Secular Reason* (Oxford, U.K.: Basil Blackwell, 1990). One passage is particularly relevant to the point made in this section:

> Religions *may* conceal historical contingency and the role of human invention, but just as often this is true of modern secular systems of thought, which are unable to admit their own choice of values with respect to the conjunction of empty freedom with an instrumentalist reason. Such an admission requires on the part of secular thought a nihilist courage, whereas, it is much *easier* for religious societies to own up to the contingency and singularity of their fundamental choices, for religions themselves acknowledge that these are not fully explicable, but wrapped up in mystery and the requirements of "faith." Just at the point of their greatest obscurity, where they most seem to invite a scientific suspicion, religions are more realistic about the inexplicable character of cultural existence than science normally dares to be. (p. 136)

The quote from Lesslie Newbigin comes from his superb book *The Gospel in a Pluralist Society* (Grand Rapids, Mich.: Eerdmans, 1989), p. 46.

Given the vigorous debate over the term *postmodernity,* I attempt no precise definition. I certainly am not baptizing the work of self-conscious and "doctrinaire" postmodernists such as Jacques Derrida and Michel Foucault. I am pointing to the cultural manifestations of what is more and more called "postmodernity" rather than to the rarefied postmodernist philosophical arguments carried on in our universities. Pressed to be more precise about what I mean by cultural postmodernity, I would identify at least seven characteristics:

1. The social construction of reality. There is a heightened, and more and more pervasive, awareness that everyone perceives or construes the world through their cultural and historical location, and this makes a difference in how we "construct" reality.

2. *A sharp increase in the rate and amount of cultural change.* The cultures of high technology and mass media change more frequently and rapidly than any cultures before them.

3. *The proliferation of choice.* More aware of cultural and social influence on what people believe and do, and how rapidly cultures change, we are freer to choose everything from deodorants to religions.

4. *Antifoundationalism.* Philosophically, and to a growing degree in popular culture, many people now accept that there is no acultural and timeless certainty about knowledge of anything; there are no foundational truths that are universally, self-evidently and noninferentially true for any rational, decent person.

5. *Suspicion of rigidly or precisely defined categories.* Given points 1-4, people doubt categories or definitions that are supposed to capture reality tightly, once and for all.

6. *Increased irony.* More aware of the social construction of reality, we sense we could be wrong about the things that matter most to us—consequently, we are more likely to hold beliefs with detachment or an air of irony.

7. *Increased awareness of differences and the "other."* Living in a mass media, technologically shrunken world, we are more intimate with people who differ from us religiously, sexually, racially, culturally and so forth.

For an understanding of postmodernity, besides books already mentioned, I have relied on Thomas C. Oden, *Two Worlds: Notes on the Death of Modernity in Russia and America* (Downers Grove, Ill.: InterVarsity Press, 1991), and *After Modernity . . . What?* (Grand Rapids, Mich.: Zondervan, 1990); Walter Truett Anderson, *Reality Isn't*

What It Used to Be (San Francisco: Harper & Row, 1990); Darrell
Jodock, *The Church's Bible* (Minneapolis: Fortress, 1989), especially
pp. 71-88; George Lindbeck, *The Nature of Doctrine* (Philadelphia:
Westminster Press, 1984); John Howard Yoder, *The Priestly Kingdom*
(Notre Dame, Ind.: University of Notre Dame Press, 1984); Donald
Allen and George F. Buttrick, eds., *The Postmoderns: The New Poetry
Revised* (New York: Grove, 1982); Paolo Portoghesi, *Postmodern: The
Architecture of the Postindustrial Society* (New York: Rizzoli, 1983);
Charles Jencks, *Post-Modernism: The New Classicism in Art and Ar-
chitecture* (New York: Rizzoli, 1987); Lawrence Grossberg, *It's a Sin:
Essays on Postmodernism, Politics and Culture* (Sydney, Australia:
Power Publications, 1988); Jeffrey Stout, *Ethics After Babel* (Boston:
Beacon, 1988); Ihab Hassan, *The Postmodern Turn: Essays in Postmod-
ern Theory and Culture* (Columbus: Ohio State University, 1987);
Stanley Hauerwas, *After Christendom?* (Nashville: Abingdon, 1991),
especially pp. 133-61, and *The Peaceable Kingdom* (Notre Dame, Ind.:
University of Notre Dame Press, 1983); John McGowan, *Postmod-
ernism and Its Critics* (Ithaca, N.Y.: Cornell University Press, 1991);
Anthony Giddens, *The Consequences of Modernity* (Stanford, Calif.:
Stanford University Press, 1990); Kenneth J. Gergen, *The Saturated
Self* (New York: BasicBooks, 1991); Jean-François Lyotard, *The Post-
modern Condition*, trans. Geoff Bennington and Drian Massumi (Min-
neapolis: University of Minnesota Press, 1984); Albert Borgmann,
Crossing the Postmodern Divide (Chicago: University of Chicago
Press, 1992); and, again, William Placher, *Unapologetic Theology*
(Louisville, Ky.: Westminster/John Knox, 1989); and David Harvey,
The Condition of Postmodernity (London: Basil Blackwell, 1989).
Among these, for understanding the cultural manifestations of postmod-
ernism, I especially recommend the volumes by Newbigin, Stout,
McGowan, Placher, Harvey, Gergen, Borgmann and Anderson.

Perhaps the most immediate and keen issue raised by postmodernity is the issue of relativism. For an excellent demonstration that there are even ancient resources for living contextually without submitting to chaotic relativism, see Martha C. Nussbaum, "The Discernment of Perception: An Aristotleian Conception of Private and Public Rationality," in *Love's Knowledge* (New York: Oxford University Press, 1990), pp. 54-105. And though they have not, so far as I am aware, spoken explicitly of postmodernity, those evangelicals developing and extending a Reformed epistemology are providing extraordinary guidance for Christians in postmodernity. See, for example, Alvin Plantinga and Nicholas Wolterstorff, eds., *Faith and Rationality* (Notre Dame, Ind.: University of Notre Dame Press, 1983); and Roy A. Clouser, *The Myth of Religious Neutrality* (Notre Dame, Ind.: University of Notre Dame Press, 1991). A fine introduction to Reformed epistemology is Kelly James Clark, *Return to Reason,* tellingly subtitled *A Critique of Enlightenment Evidentialism and a Defense of Reason and Belief in God* (Grand Rapids, Mich.: Eerdmans, 1990). Alan Jacobs is another evangelical critiquing "Enlightenment evidentialism," though not from an explicitly Reformed perspective. See his "Rhetoric and the Task of Apologetics in Contemporary America," *Proceedings of the Wheaton Theology Conference,* Spring 1992, pp. 163-73.

CHAPTER 2: The Unnaturalness of Family

Winwood Reade's adventures are recounted in Paul G. Hiebert, *Cultural Anthropology* (Grand Rapids, Mich.: Baker Book House, 1983), pp. 26-27.

The Family: The Bourgeois Model

The characteristics of bourgeois family are from Brigitte Berger and Peter L. Berger, *The War over the Family* (Garden City, N.Y.: Doubleday, 1983), pp. 101-2. I have relied heavily on the excellent chapter on the traditionalist family (coauthored with Helen V. L. Stehlin) in James Davison Hunter's *Evangelicalism: The Coming Generation* (Chicago: University of Chicago Press, 1987), pp. 76-115. Here follows the data on the traditionalist books cited in this section: Rus Walton, *One Nation Under God* (Old Tappan, N.J.: Revell, 1975), pp. 85 and 99; Kenneth Chafin, *Is There a Family in the House?* (Waco, Tex.: Word Books, 1978), p. 158; Larry Christenson, *The Christian Family* (Minneapolis: Bethany House, 1970), pp. 61-62 (emphasis mine); James Dobson, *Straight Talk to Men and Their Wives* (Waco, Tex.: Word Books, 1982), p. 21; Gene A. Getz, *The Measure of a Family* (Ventura, Calif.: Regal Books, 1976); Dan Benson, *Total Man* (Wheaton, Ill.: Tyndale House, 1981); Jennifer Logan, *Not Just Any Man: A Practical Guide to Finding Mr. Right* (Dallas: Word Books, 1988); and Michael Brown, *The Christian in an Age of Sexual Eclipse* (Wheaton, Ill.: Tyndale House, 1983).

On Tocqueville and the Protestant idealization of femininity, see Randall Balmer, *Mine Eyes Have Seen the Glory: A Journey into the Evangelical Subculture in America* (New York: Oxford University Press, 1989), pp. 118-22. George Gilder's *Sexual Suicide* has been republished as *Men and Marriage* (New York: Pelican, 1986). For appreciative traditionalist evangelical responses, see the review by Jan Dennis, "Civilizing the Sexual Barbarians," *Christianity Today,* March 6, 1987, pp. 35-36; and James Robison, *Attack on the Family* (Wheaton, Ill.: Tyndale House, 1982), pp. 24-25.

The Unbiblical Israelite Family
For information on the Israelite household, my sources include Hans Walter Wolff, *Anthropology of the Old Testament* (Philadelphia: Fortress, 1974); Norman K. Gottwald, *The Tribes of Yahweh* (Maryknoll, N.Y.: Orbis Books, 1979); Raphael Patai, *Sex and Family in the Bible and the Middle East* (Garden City, N.Y.: Doubleday, 1959); Harry A. Hoffner, "Bayith," in *Theological Dictionary of the Old Testament,* ed. G. Johannes Botterweck

and Helmer Ringgren, trans. John T. Willis (Grand Rapids, Mich.: Eerdmans, 1975), 2:113; R. K. Bower and G. L. Knapp, "Marriage, Marry," in *The International Standard Bible Encyclopedia,* ed. Geoffrey W. Bromiley (Grand Rapids, Mich.: Eerdmans, 1986), 3:262, and "Relationships, Family," in the same work, 4:75-79. On David's marriage alliances, see John Bright, *A History of Israel* (Philadelphia: Westminster Press, 1981), pp. 193, 197 and 198 (whence the quote). The quote from Thomas Martin is found in his *Christian Family Values* (New York: Paulist, 1984), p. 48.

If We Did What Came Naturally, Would There Be Families?

On the three universal traits of family, see Hiebert, *Cultural Anthropology,* pp. 196-97; and Michael C. Howard, *Contemporary Cultural Anthropology* (Boston: Little, Brown, 1986), pp. 214-15. On "women's ways of knowing" and the differences between women and men, see Carol Gilligan, *A Different Voice: Psychological Theory and Women's Development* (Cambridge, Mass.: Harvard University Press, 1982); Catherine Keller, *From a Broken Web: Separation, Sexism and Self*; and, for a superb evangelical discussion, Mary Stewart Van Leeuwen, *Gender and Grace: Love, Work and Parenting in a Changing World* (Downers Grove, Ill.: InterVarsity Press, 1990). At present there are fewer books trying to attain a better understanding of masculinity, but see James Nelson, *The Intimate Connection: Male Sexuality, Masculine Spirituality* (Philadelphia: Westminster Press, 1988); Verne Becker, *The Real Man Inside* (Grand Rapids, Mich.: Zondervan, 1992); and Jack Balswick, *Men at the Crossroads* (Downers Grove, Ill.: InterVarsity Press, 1992).

As reflected in my main text, the third of these three "natural" characteristics of family is the least certain or easily specifiable. Clearly we all have much to learn about the real differences and similarities between men and women. In any event, I accept the distinction between sex and gender. Sex is a biological category identifying the physiologically male and physiologically female. Gender is a social category identifying how a particular culture expects physiological males to be masculine and physiological females to be feminine. The relativity of gender makes the discussion of "true manhood" and "true womanhood" exceedingly tricky. Besides Van Leeuwen's *Gender and Grace,* one of the most helpful and lucid discussions I have come across is Alistair I. McFadyen, *The Call to Personhood* (Cambridge, U.K.: Cambridge University Press, 1990), pp. 31-39.

Naturally, But Not Instinctually

On the importance of culture to the development of persons, see Peter L. Berger and Thomas Luckmann, *The Social Construction of Reality* (New York: Anchor/Doubleday, 1966), pp. 47-50, 136-37 and 181. Equally important is Clifford Geertz, *The Interpretation of Culture* (New York: Basic Books, 1973), pp. 33-54. On the matter of what I have called "social necessity," see Basil Mitchell, Morality: Religious and Secular (Oxford, U.K.: Clarendon, 1980); and Paul Nelson, Narrative and Morality: A Theological Inquiry (University Park, Penn.: Pennsylvania State University Press, 1987).

It may be worth pointing out that if there is no such thing as pure or acultural rationality, neither (as the Romantic tradition would have it) is there pure or acultural emotion. For instance, see the fascinating essay by philosopher Martha Nussbaum in which she shows "that emotions are not feelings that well up in some natural and untutored way from our natural selves, that they are, in fact, not personal or natural at all, that they are, instead, contrivances, social constructs. We learn how to feel, and we learn our emotional repertoire. We learn emotions in the same way that we learn our beliefs—from our society." See "Narrative Emotions: Beckett's Genealogy of Love," in *Love's Knowledge* (New York: Oxford University Press, 1990), pp. 286-313 (quote from p. 287). See also Kenneth J. Gergen, *The Saturated Self* (New

York: BasicBooks, 1991), pp. 8-10 and 164-66. For profound theological comment on these realities, see Nicholas Lash, *Easter in Ordinary*
(Notre Dame, Ind.: University of Notre Dame Press, 1988), especially
pp. 60-64.

Of Seuss and the Kingdom
In this section I have leaned heavily on John Howard Yoder, *The Christian
Witness to the State* (Newton, Kans.: Faith and Life, 1964), especially pp.
33-35 and 79-82; and *The Priestly Kingdom: Social Ethics as Gospel* (Notre
Dame, Ind.: University of Notre Dame Press, 1984). Beyond price is Oliver
O'Donovan's discussion of creation and kingdom ethics—so often pitted
against one another—in *Resurrection and Moral Order: An Outline for
Evangelical Ethics* (Grand Rapids, Mich.: Eerdmans, 1986), pp. 31-97. An
extraordinary treatment of "nature" in Romans is Richard B. Hays, "Rela-
tions Natural and Unnatural: A Response to John Boswell's Exegesis of
Romans 1," *The Journal of Religious Ethics* 14 (Spring 1986): 184-215.
Finally, I wrote with one other discussion of "nature" and natural theology
in mind. That was Wolfgang Schrage, *The Ethics of the New Testament,* trans.
David E. Green (Philadelphia: Fortress, 1988), pp. 201-3.

CHAPTER 3: Advanced Capitalism & the Lost Art of Christian Family
Novelist Don DeLillo is one of the keenest observers of the madder side of
contemporary America. Among his several books, see *White Noise* (New
York: Penguin, 1984), *Americana* (New York: Penguin, 1971) and *Players*
(New York: Vintage, 1977).

A Suburban Exile
Much has been written on the fragmentation of life endemic to urban and
suburban existence. Especially clarifying for me has been the work of
Alasdair MacIntyre, *After Virtue: A Study in Moral Theory,* 2nd ed. (Notre

Dame, Ind.: University of Notre Dame Press, 1984). An excellent summary of that book is found in the first chapter of MacIntyre's later work *Whose Justice? Which Rationality?* (Notre Dame, Ind.: University of Notre Dame Press, 1988). Also helpful, and along similar lines, is the initial chapter of Stanley Hauerwas's *The Peaceable Kingdom: A Primer in Christian Ethics* (Notre Dame, Ind.: University of Notre Dame Press, 1983). MacIntyre and Hauerwas have recognized that the problem of fragmentation is profoundly mutilating our lives. They are helping us to see how important such "ordinary" and supposedly private things as family and friendship are to faith and morality. Along these lines, consult the fine book by Paul J. Wadell, *Friendship and the Moral Life* (Notre Dame: University of Notre Dame Press, 1989).

A host of sociologists explore the dilemmas of fragmentation and pluralization. I would mention Peter Berger, *The Heretical Imperative* (Garden City, N.Y.: Anchor, 1979), and *A Far Glory* (New York: Free Press, 1992); and Os Guinness, *The Gravedigger File: Papers on the Subversion of the Modern Church* (Downers Grove, Ill.: InterVarsity Press, 1983).

What Really Ails the Family

For the common blacklist of Christian family advocates, see, e.g., Tim LaHaye, *The Battle for the Family* (Old Tappan, N.J.: Revell, 1982).

Historian Stephanie Coontz corroborates a point that is one of the central contentions of this chapter (and entire book): on its own and isolated, the nuclear family cannot successfully resist the irresponsibility and immorality so pervasive in our society. Coontz understands why so many people yearn for the restoration of "family values." But, she writes,

> very few people can sustain values at a personal level when they are continually contradicted at work, at the store, in the government and on

television. To call their failure to do so a family crisis is much like calling pneumonia a breathing crisis. Certainly, pneumonia affects people's ability to breathe easily, but telling them to start breathing properly again ... is not going to cure the disease. The crisis of the family ... is in many ways a larger crisis of *social* reproduction: a major upheaval in the way we produce, reproduce and distribute goods, services, power, economic rewards and social roles.

See her "On the Edge," *Chicago Tribune Magazine,* October 11, 1992, pp. 13-21 (quote from p. 21).

I mention that abuse may be as prevalent—or even more prevalent—in Christian homes as in the general population. For one sobering example see Peter Nicolai et al., Report of the Synodical Committee on Physical, Emotional, and Sexual Abuse in the Christian Reformed Church (September, 1991). See also James Alsdurf and Phyllis Alsdurf, *Battered into Submission* (Downers Grove, Ill.: InterVarsity Press, 1989).

Key influences on my reading of Scripture and the church-culture relationship include Jacques Ellul, *The Subversion of Christianity,* trans. Geoffrey W. Bromiley (Grand Rapids, Mich.: Eerdmans, 1986); James Wm. McClendon Jr., *Systematic Theology: Ethics* (Nashville: Abingdon, 1986), especially pp. 160-239; Stanley Hauerwas, *Against the Nations: War and Survival in a Liberal Society* (Minneapolis: Seabury, 1985), especially pp. 107-32, and *Christian Existence Today: Essays on Church, World and Living In Between* (Durham, N.C.: Labyrinth, 1988); Karl Barth, *Church Dogmatics,* particularly 4/2, trans. G. W. Bromiley (Edinburgh: T. & T. Clark, 1958), pp. 533-53; Vernard Eller, *Christian Anarchy: Jesus' Primacy over the Powers* (Grand Rapids, Mich.: Eerdmans, 1987); and John Howard Yoder, *The Original Revolution: Essays on Christian Pacifism* (Scottdale, Penn.: Herald, 1971), and *The Politics of Jesus: Vicit Agnus Noster* (Grand Rapids, Mich.: Eerdmans, 1972). More of my understanding of these issues is spelled out in Robert E. Webber and Rodney Clapp, *People of the Truth: The Power of the Worshiping Community in the Modern World* (San Francisco: Harper & Row, 1988; Harrisburg, Penn.: Morehouse, 1993).

I am sensitive that when I declare the task of the church is to live true to the kingdom "under whatever governmental and economic system," some readers (especially neoconservatives) may think I am subscribing to the doctrine of "moral equivalency"—that all worldly systems are equally good or evil. I am not. Clearly Marxist-Leninism, for example, was a political-economic system responsible for more human suffering than many other systems. My point is that the church must live and act critically in every cultural setting. There is a crucial place for discerning what system immediately available is most good or least evil. But I fear American Christians too often fall into the error of assuming we cannot criticize our system unless we can first present a full-scale substitute for it. I suspect that beneath this error lie two more basic errors: (1) A Constantianian bias, the feeling that Christians are responsible to manage the course of history and make the world come out right. But that is not our confession. Our confession is that God is God, and will make the world come out right. The church's responsibility is not to manage the world but to witness to the world the reality of God's kingdom. (2) The pervasive but illusory importance of government in modern times. Since the rise of the nation-state, government has been assumed to be the answer to all problems. As Robert Nisbet notes, we betray our presumption of government's signal importance when we look at anything wrong and then immediately ask, "What can government do about it?" (*The Present Age* [New York: Harper & Row, 1988]). Even conservative Christians have fallen into this trap. By contrast, biblically the social agent of God's salvation is the church, not the nation-state.

Yahweh as a Household God

Steven Mintz and Susan Kellogg are quoted from their *Domestic Revolutions: A Social History of American Family Life* (New York: Free Press, 1988), p. xv. Ellis, Bushnell and Ruskin are all cited in Bram Dijkstra, *Idols of Perversity* (New York: Oxford University Press, 1986), pp. 10-13. The material on women and shopping is also found in Dijkstra, pp. 362-67. I quote Donald Meyer from his *The Positive Thinkers* (Middletown, Conn.: Wesleyan University Press, 1988), p. 54. For corroborating documentation and insights, particularly regarding the split between public and private, see Elizabeth Fox-Genovese, *Feminism Without Illusions* (Chapel Hill, N.C.: University of North Carolina Press, 1991).

The Belligerence of the Bottom Line

Victor Lebow is cited in Alan Durning, "How Much Is Enough?" *Utne Reader*, July/August, 1991, p. 73 (emphasis mine).

The dominance of the market mentality is more and more widely recognized. It is important to emphasize that criticisms of this development come from across the ideological spectrum, not simply from leftists. Those deploring this development include George F. Will, *Statecraft as Soulcraft* (New York: Simon and Schuster, 1983); Robert Nisbet, *The Present Age;* Glenn Tinder, *The Political Meaning of Christianity* (Baton Rouge: Louisiana State University Press, 1989), p. 12; Allan C. Carlson, *From Cottage to Work Station* (San Francisco: Ignatius, 1993); Robert N. Bellah et al., *Habits of the Heart: Individualism and Commitment in American Life* (Berkeley: University of California Press, 1985); Cornel West, *Prophetic Fragments* (Grand Rapids, Mich.: Eerdmans, 1988); Charles K. Wilber and Laura Grimes, "The Moral Defense of Market Capitalism: A Critique of the Literature," paper delivered at a September 8-10, 1987, conference at Wheaton College, Biblical Perspectives on a Mixed Market Economy; Stephanie

Coontz, *The Way We Never Were* (New York: BasicBooks, 1992); Jeffrey Stout, *Ethics After Babel: The Languages of Morals and Their Discontents* (Boston: Beacon, 1988), pp. 191-292; MacIntyre, *After Virtue;* Stanley Hauerwas, *A Community of Character: Toward a Constructive Christian Social Ethic* (Notre Dame, Ind.: University of Notre Dame Press, 1981); Michael Walzer, *Spheres of Justice: A Defense of Pluralism and Equality* (New York: BasicBooks, 1983), especially pp. 95-128; Barbara Ehrenreich, *Fear of Falling: The Inner Life of the Middle Class* (New York: Pantheon, 1989); and John Francis Kavanaugh, *Following Christ in a Consumer Society: The Spirituality of Cultural Resistance* (Maryknoll, N.Y.: Orbis Books, 1981). *Marketing Your Ministry* is authored by John W. Pearson and Robert D. Hirsch (Brentwood, Tenn.: Wolgemuth & Hyatt, 1990). For documentation and insightful criticism of several other writers who believe the church should adopt marketing tactics, see Douglas Webster, *Selling Jesus* (Downers Grove, Ill.: InterVarsity Press, 1992). I discuss the marketization of friendship at more length in "The Celebration of Friendship," *The Reformed Journal*, August 1989, pp. 11-13. On Milton Friedman and the Chicago school of economics, see Alan Wolfe, *Whose Keeper? Social Science and Moral Obligation* (Berkeley: University of California Press, 1989), pp. 31-32, 38.

When Heaven Is a Supermarket

The statistics on the number of products in supermarkets and so forth come from Steven Waldman, "The Tyranny of Choice," *The New Republic,* January 27, 1992, pp. 22-25. Robert Webber discusses the variety of evangelicals in *Common Roots* (Grand Rapids, Mich.: Zondervan, 1978), p. 32.

Family in the Image of the Market

No one is more perspicacious than Hauerwas on this subject. See especially

A *Community of Character,* pp. 155-95. Also speaking critically of family molded along the lines of economic exchange are Philip Turner, *Sex, Money and Power: An Essay in Christian Social Ethics* (Cambridge, Mass.: Cowley Books, 1985); and Timothy F. Sedgwick, *Sacramental Ethics: Paschal Identity and the Christian Life* (Philadelphia: Fortress, 1987). Other insights in this section were drawn from Eli Zaretsky, *Capitalism, the Family and Personal Life* (New York: Harper & Row, 1986). The Nisbet quote comes from Robert Nisbet, *The Quest for Community: A Study in the Ethics of Order and Freedom* (New York: Oxford University Press, 1953), p. 61.

Two Visions

I do not refer flippantly to story and its power to shape our identity. Narrative's necessity to our personhood has been set forth by Christian philosophers such as Alasdair MacIntyre *(After Virtue)* and Charles Taylor, *Sources of the Self: The Making of the Modern Identity* (Cambridge, Mass.: Harvard University Press, 1989). Psychologists are also speaking of the necessity of narrative to the formation of self. See, for instance, Jerome Bruner, *Actual Minds, Possible Worlds* (Cambridge, Mass.: Harvard University Press, 1986); and Erving Polster, *Every Person's Life Is Worth a Novel* (New York: W. W. Norton, 1987). In theology, the literature is immense, but for introductions see George W. Stroup, *The Promise of Narrative Theology* (Atlanta: John Knox, 1981); and Terrence W. Tilley, *Story Theology* (Wilmington, Del.: Michael Glazier, 1985). A recent evangelical endorsement of narrative theology comes from Clark H. Pinnock, *Tracking the Maze: Finding Our Way Through Modern Theology from an Evangelical Perspective* (San Francisco: Harper & Row, 1990), pp. 153-222. Richard J. Mouw also provides an excellent evangelical assessment of narrative theology in chapter 7 of *The God Who Commands* (Notre Dame, Ind.: University of Notre Dame Press, 1990), pp. 116-49. Some evangelicals are concerned that narrative theology leads to a tendency to dismiss the historical referents of biblical narrative. For a compelling argument that this need not at all be the case, see evangelical scholar N. T. Wright's *The New Testament and the People of God* (Minneapolis: Fortress, 1992), pp. xvii, 47-144, 372.

CHAPTER 4: Church as First Family

I quote R. J. Rushdoony from his *Salvation and Godly Rule* (Vallecito, Calif.: Ross House, 1983), p. 477 (emphasis mine). For another evangelical traditionalist approach that makes biological family central, see William Pride and Mary Pride, "Marriage and Family," in *Applying the Scriptures,* ed. Kenneth Kantzer (Grand Rapids, Mich.: Zondervan, 1987), pp. 187-217.

On the Gospel of John as the church's primary creation account, I borrow from Paul Ramsey. In his exact words, "The Prologue of St. John's Gospel is the Christian story of creation, our chief creation story, primary over Genesis, as John 1:3 states." See Ramsey's *Speak Up for Just War or Pacifism,* with an epilogue by Stanley Hauerwas (University Park, Penn.: Pennsylvania State University Press, 1988), p. 21.

The Centrality of Covenant

Folksinger Raffi's song is "All I Really Need," from the album *Baby Beluga* (Troubador Records, 1980). On bachelorhood and the status of eunuchs, see Marcus J. Borg, *Jesus: A New Vision* (San Francisco: Harper & Row, 1987), p. 122, n. 75; and Bruce J. Malina, *The New Testament World: Insights from Cultural Anthropology* (Atlanta: John Knox Press, 1981), p. 133. L. William Countryman is quoted from his *Dirt, Greed and Sex: Sexual Ethics in the New Testament and Their Implications for Today* (Philadelphia: Fortress, 1988), p. 169. On procreation and rabbinical views, see O. Larry Yarbrough, *Not Like the Gentiles: Marriage Rules in the Letters of Paul* (Atlanta: Scholars, 1985), pp. 21-23. For Barth on marriage in the Old Testament, see Karl Barth, *Church Dogmatics,* 3/4, trans. A. T. Mackay et al. (Edinburgh: T. & T. Clark, 1961), pp. 197-98.

Can Bachelors Keep the Covenant?

On covenant as a historical and theological matter rather than one of kinship, see John Bright, *A History of Israel*, 3rd ed. (Philadelphia: Westminister Press, 1981), p. 163. The connection between obedience and the covenant is spelled out in Edwyn Clement Hoskyns and Francis Noel Davey, *Crucifixion-Resurrection: The Pattern of Theology and Ethics in the New Testament* (London: SPCK, 1981). I quote singer Bruce Cockburn from his song "Indian Wars," on the album *Nothing But a Burning Light* (Columbia, 1991).

How Kingdom Threatens the Family

The view of the kingdom summarized here is that presented by a wide consensus of scholars. For evangelical treatments of the subject, see George Eldon Ladd, *The Presence of the Future* (Grand Rapids, Mich.: Eerdmans, 1974); Allen Verhey, *The Great Reversal: Ethics and the New Testament* (Grand Rapids, Mich.: Eerdmans, 1984); C. René Padilla, *Mission Between the Times: Essays on the Kingdom* (Grand Rapids, Mich.: Eerdmans, 1985); Christopher J. H. Wright, *An Eye for an Eye* (Downers Grove, Ill.: InterVarsity Press, 1983); Mark Strom, *The Symphony of Scripture* (Downers Grove, Ill.: InterVarsity Press, 1990); and John Howard Yoder, *The Original Revolution: Essays on Christian Pacifism* (Scottdale, Penn.: Herald Press, 1971). In the latter book (p. 55), Yoder concisely describes the perspective I mean to represent:

> The New Testament sees our present age—the age of the church, extending from Pentecost to the Parousia—as a period of the overlapping of two aeons. These aeons are not distinct periods of time, for they exist simultaneously. They differ rather in nature or in direction; one points backwards to human history outside of (before) Christ; the other points forward to the fullness of the kindgom of God, of which it is a foretaste. Each aeon has a social manifestation: the former in the "world," the latter in the church or the body of Christ.

First Family Is the Church

It is a salutary rebuke to the church's overvaluing of family to remember that Jesus was seen as a family-breaker. There are ironies in the church's frequent attacks on such so-called cults as Sun Myung Moon's Unification Church and the Mormons.

One irony is that the early Christians were the Moonies of their day. They were hated because the allegiances they demanded from converts sometimes conflicted with family allegiances. A Roman family might, for instance, worship a number of popular gods—especially those in favor with the ruling elite at the time. It could be financially and politically costly to worship a single, imperious god, such as the God of Israel and Jesus. So if a Roman son became a Christian, the entire family fortune and heritage were endangered. The resulting conflicts were severe. Families were actually divided.

A second irony is quite different. In their own ways Moonies and Mormons affirm the biological family in a manner very close to traditionalist evangelicals. That is, traditionalists tend to see the family as God's premier social agent on earth, the central vehicle of salvation. So do Moonies and Mormons. The Mormons, of course, are famous for the promotion of family life and their expectation (contrary to Mk 12:25 and parallels) that marriage will continue into eternity. (See Allan C. Carlson, *From Cottage to Work Station* [San Francisco: Ignatius, 1993], pp. 92-93.) It is less well known that Sun Myung Moon sees the effects of original sin reversed through the marriage and childbearing of the true Messiah. For Moon, Jesus failed as the Messiah because he got himself killed before he could marry and have children. (See J. Gordon Melton, "What's Behind the Moonie Mass Marriages," *Christianity Today,* December 16, 1983, pp. 28-31.)

Evangelical traditionalists do not see marriage extending into eternity and do not, of course, think Jesus failed because he did not marry

and father a family. In a way, then, evangelical traditionalists actually
value the biological family *less* than Mormons and Moonies. I suspect
that is the case exactly because traditionalists are truer to Scripture than
Mormons or Moonies.

On respecting parents by attending to their burial, see Francis Wright
Beare, *The Gospel According to Matthew* (San Francisco: Harper &
Row, 1987), p. 214. On the significance of Jesus' words against divorce,
see Richard A. Horsley, *Jesus and the Spiral of Violence: Popular
Jewish Resistance in Roman Palestine* (San Francisco: Harper & Row,
1987), p. 236. On corban, see Ben Witherington III, *Women and the
Genesis of Christianity* (Cambridge, U.K.: Cambridge University Press,
1990), pp. 29-31.

For additional theological corroboration of this section, see Ray S.
Anderson and Dennis B. Guernsey, *On Being Family: A Social Theol-
ogy of the Family* (Grand Rapids, Mich.: Eerdmans, 1985), particularly
chapters 2 and 11; and Bruce J. Malina and Richard L. Rohrbaugh,
Social-Science Commentary on the Synoptic Gospels (Minneapolis:
Fortress, 1992), pp. 99-101. Other theological studies addressing the
family (and not noted elsewhere in this book) include Elisabeth
Schüssler Fiorenza, *In Memory of Her* (New York: Crossroad, 1983);
Vigen Guroian, *Incarnate Love: Essays in Orthodox Ethics* (Notre
Dame, Ind.: University of Notre Dame Press, 1987), pp. 79-114; James
Gustafson, *Ethics from a Theocentric Perspective* (Chicago: University
of Chicago Press, 1984), 2:153-84; Roger Mehl, *Society and Love:
Ethical Problems of Family Life,* trans. James H. Farley (Philadelphia:
Westminster Press, 1964); James H. Olthuis, *I Pledge You My Troth: A
Christian View of Marriage, Family, Friendship* (New York: Harper &
Row, 1975); Janet Fishburn, *Confronting the Idolatry of Family* (Nash-
ville: Abingdon, 1991); Eduard Schillebeeckx, *Marriage: Secular Re-
ality and Saving Mystery,* trans. N. D. Smith (London: Sheed and Ward,

1965); William H. Willimon, *The Service of God* (Nashville: Abingdon, 1983), pp. 170-86; and Diogenes Allen, *Love: Christian Romance, Marriage, Friendship* (Cambridge, Mass.: Cowley, 1987).

Mary: Mother or Disciple First?

There are many helpful readings of the Mark 3 passage, but see especially Ched Myers, *Binding the Strong Man: A Political Reading of Mark's Story of Jesus* (Maryknoll, N.Y.: Orbis Books, 1988), pp. 167-68. Jesus' delivery of his mother to a new family at his crucifixion is suggested by David E. Garland and Diana R. Garland, "The Family: Biblical and Theological Perspectives," in *Incarnational Ministry: The Presence of Christ in Church, Society and Family,* ed. Christian D. Kettler and Todd H. Speidell (Colorado Springs, Colo.: Helmers & Howard, 1990), pp. 230-31; and by Countryman, *Dirt, Greed and Sex,* p. 186.

Paul's First Family

On the importance of family language to Paul, see Robert Banks, *Paul's Idea of Community: The Early House Churches in Their Historical Setting* (Grand Rapids, Mich.: Eerdmans, 1980), pp. 52-54; and Wayne A. Meeks, *The First Urban Christians: The Social World of the Apostle Paul* (New Haven, Conn.: Yale University Press, 1983), pp. 86-87. On the capacity of homes in Paul's day, see Banks, pp. 41-42. On adoption in Paul, see also Meeks, *First Urban Christians*, pp. 88 and 184; and Meeks, *The Moral World of the First Christians* (Philadelphia: Westminster Press, 1986), pp. 126 and 129. See also Malina, *New Testament World*, pp. 109-16. For the Greer citation, see Rowan A. Greer, *Broken Lights and Mended Lives* (University Park, Penn.: Pennsylvania State University Press, 1986), pp. 103-4. For the Wright citation, see again *The New Testament and the People of God,* pp. 449-50. And for the Nisbet quote, see Robert A. Nisbet, *The Social Philosophers* (New York: Washington Square Press, 1973), pp. 80-81.

An excellent summary of the biblical evidence I have tried to adduce in this and the previous two sections is found in the words of ethicist and biblical scholar Thomas Ogletree:

In postexilic Judaism, as in ancient Israel, the family is foundational for the existence of the people. The community of faith is constituted through the joining of families in covenant. In this respect the Jewish community might be called a natural community, that is, a community emerging out of the propagation and socialization of offspring. For Christian understanding, the family is secondary and derivative; the community of faith, primary and fundamental. The community of faith is in its essence a gathered community. It lives and grows by way of an evangelistic witness. The witness is directed not to families, but to individual persons, Jew and gentile, slave and free, male and female.

See *The Use of the Bible in Christian Ethics* (Philadelphia: Fortress, 1983), pp. 181-82.

A Genuine Reconciliation

Throughout this section I have relied heavily on John D. Zizioulas, *Being as Communion: Studies in Personhood and the Church* (Crestwood, N.Y.: St. Vladimir's Seminary Press, 1985), especially pp. 55-59. *Da* (1988) is a film directed by Matt Clark. Karl Barth is quoted from his *Church Dogmatics,* 3/4:264.

CHAPTER 5: The Superiority of Singleness

In November 1991 the Barna Research Group polled Americans, asking them which of fifteen "people groups" were treated most sensitively by Protestant churches. The group to which churches were perceived to be most sensitive was families (46 percent of the polled said churches were "very sensitive" to families). By contrast, only 16 percent said churches were "very sensitive" to single adults, and a mere 17 percent said they were sensitive to single parents. As researcher George Barna commented, "Single parents are a growing segment of our population, with substantial physical and emotional needs, yet just over two out of ten single parents say churches are very sensitive to these needs. Research shows that single adults are considerably more likely to be lonely and in need of support from . . . the church, yet barely one out of ten single adults feels churches are very sensitive to them. . . . The people most in need of the church are the ones who feel most shunned by it." See *Single Adult Ministries Journal,* January 1992, pp. 1-2.

Isaiah Berlin is quoted from John McGowan, *Postmodernism and Its Critics* (Ithaca, N.Y.: Cornell University Press, 1991), p. 37.

Augustine's Wrong Turn

For Augustine's views on sexuality, I have in mind of course *The Confessions,* trans. John K. Ryan (Garden City, N.Y.: Doubleday, 1960) and *City of God,* trans. Gerald G. Walsh, ed. Vernon J. Burke (Garden City, N.Y.: Doubleday, 1958). I also relied on several other treatises, all found in the series The Fathers of the Church (New York: Fathers of the Church, dates ranging from 1948 to 1957): *Adulterous Marriages, Against Julian, Enchiridion, The Good of Marriage, Holy Virginity, On Marriage and Concupiscence* and *Sermons on Liturgical Seasons.*

My reading of Augustine on sex owes much to Peter Brown, *Augustine and Sexuality* (Berkeley, Calif.: Center for Hermeneutical Studies, 1983), *Augustine of Hippo* (Berkeley: University of California Press, 1967) and *The Philosopher and Society in Late Antiquity* (Berkeley, Calif.: Center for Hermeneutical Studies, 1980). It was also influenced by Margaret A. Miles, *Augustine on the Body* (Missoula, Mont.: Scholars, 1979); Lisa Sowle Cahill, *Between the Sexes* (Philadelphia: Fortress, 1985); and Samuel Laeuchli, *Power and Sexuality* (Philadelpha: Temple University Press, 1972). A somewhat more sympathetic reading of Augustine on sex is found in Garry Wills, *Under God* (New York:

Simon and Schuster, 1990), pp. 281-83.

Gregory of Nazianzus is cited in Laeuchli, pp. 104-5. I quote Plotinus from Brown, *The Philosopher and Society in Late Antiquity,* p. 1. The direct quotations of Augustine are from *Holy Virginity* 13 and 12 and *Sermons on Liturgical Seasons* 188. Luther's remarks come from Paul Althaus, *The Ethics of Martin Luther,* trans. Robert C. Schultz (Phila-del-phia: Fortress, 1972), pp. 84-88. Lord Acton is cited in William Manchester, *The Last Lion* (Boston: Little, Brown, 1983), p. 62. The quote from C. S. Lewis rests in *The Problem of Pain* (New York: Macmillan, 1962), p. 78. On shame and a proper reading of Genesis, see Walter Brueggemann, *Genesis* (Atlanta: John Knox, 1982), p. 42.

Why the Childless Were Without Joy in Zion
On Old Testament understandings of death and individual survival, see Lloyd R. Bailey Sr., *Biblical Perspectives on Death* (Philadelphia: Fortress, 1979); Lou H. Silberman, "Death in the Hebrew Bible and Apocalyptic Literature," in *Perspectives on Death,* ed. Liston O. Mills (Nashville: Abingdon, 1969), pp. 13-32; and Stanley Bruce Frost, "The Memorial of the Childless Man: A Study in Hebrew Thought on Immortality," *Interpretation* 26 (1972): 437-50. An excellent brief and accessible treatment is Allen F. Page, *Life After Death: What the Bible Says* (Nashville: Abingdon, 1987).

I cite John W. Cooper from his *Body, Soul and Life Everlasting: Biblical Anthropology and the Monism-Dualism Debate* (Grand Rapids, Mich.: Eerdmans, 1989), pp. 41, 61-62 and 66; see the whole of his treatment of Old Testament anthropology on pp. 36-80. I quote Johannes Pedersen from *Israel: Its Life and Culture,* vols. 1-2 (London: Oxford University Press, 1926), p. 245.

The Superiority of Singleness for Awkward Times
For an understanding of singleness in the New Testament, I am indebted to

Francis Wright Beare, *The Gospel According to Matthew* (San Francisco: Harper & Row, 1981); Wolfgang Schrage, *The Ethics of the New Testament*, trans. David E. Green (Philadelphia: Fortress, 1988); and several studies of 1 Corinthians, including David R. Cartlidge, "1 Corinthians 7 as a Foundation for a Christian Sex Ethic," *The Journal of Religion* 55, no. 2 (1975): 220-34; Gordon D. Fee, *The First Epistle to the Corinthians* (Grand Rapids, Mich.: Eerdmans, 1987); David E. Garland, "The Christian's Posture Toward Marriage and Celibacy: 1 Corinthians 7," *Review and Expositor* 80, no. 3 (1983): 357-62; Charles H. Talbert, *Reading Corinthians* (New York: Crossroad, 1987); Anthony C. Thistleton, "Realized Eschatology at Corinth," *New Testament Studies* 24 (1978): 510-26; and Vincent L. Wimbush, *Paul: The Worldly Ascetic* (Macon, Ga.: Mercer University Press, 1987).

Stanley Hauerwas speaks from *A Community of Character: Toward a Constructive Christian Social Ethic* (Notre Dame, Ind.: University of Notre Dame Press, 1981), p. 190.

The Odd Freedom of the New Testament

Calvin speaks from *Institutes of the Christian Religion,* ed. John T. McNeill, trans. Ford Lewis Battles (Philadelphia: Westminster Press, 1960), 1:35, n. 3. Archimandrite Kallistos Ware is the Orthodox theologian, quoted here from his *The Orthodox Way* (Crestwood, N.Y.: St. Vladimir's Seminary Press, 1979), p. 72.

Oliver O'Donovan offers some helpful insight on the complementary witness of singleness and family in his *Resurrection and Moral Order: An Outline for Evangelical Ethics* (Grand Rapids, Mich.: Eerdmans, 1986), pp. 70-71.

The Variety of Christian Freedoms

I quote Camille Paglia from her *Sexual Personae* (New Haven, Conn.: Yale University Press, 1990), p. 234.

Kenneth Gergen is quoted in Steven Waldman, "The Tyranny of Choice," *The New Republic,* January 22, 1992, pp. 22-25. Several other postmodern commentators discuss schizophrenia. See, for instance, Fredric Jameson, *Postmodernism: Or, The Cultural Logic of Late Capitalism* (Durham, N.C.: Duke University Press, 1991). But I am especially indebted to the acute remarks of John McGowan in *Postmodernism and Its Critics* (Ithaca, N.Y.: Cornell University Press, 1991), pp. 246-47. My account of integrated selfhood, besides attempting to be true to the biblical story, is drawn from Josiah Royce, *The Philosophy of Loyalty* (New York: Macmillan, 1908), and the wonderful work of H. Richard Niebuhr, especially *The Responsible Self: An Essay in Christian Moral Philosophy* (San Francisco: Harper & Row, 1963) and *Faith on Earth: An Inquiry into the Structure of Human Faith* (New Haven, Conn.: Yale University Press, 1989).

Lewis Smedes writes on cross-sexual friendships in *Mere Morality: What God Expects from Ordinary People* (Grand Rapids, Mich.: Eerdmans, 1983), pp. 169-72. On this matter, I heartily affirm the words of Philip Turner:

> Beneath our disordered desires lies a loneliness brought about by a failure in the common life God intends for all men and women. The churches in America in many ways simply contribute to this loneliness. Their common life too frequently is not formed as a society of friends who share one Lord, one Faith and one Baptism. It is rather formed around the needs and expectations of the bourgeois family. Single people are at best tolerated. Nevertheless, the view that sexual relations are intended for marital rather than general social relations is linked to the idea that close bonds between men and women, both single and married, ought to exist in all of life's dimensions. Because of these bonds, sexual relations themselves are not necessary as a cure for loneliness. What is necessary is the fellowship of men and women in Christ. This is the word beyond "no" the church has

to speak to single people.

See "Sex and the Single Life," *First Things,* May 1993, p. 20.

Christopher Lasch talks about limits and the illusiveness of progress in his *The True and Only Heaven* (New York: W. W. Norton, 1991).

John Updike discusses psoriasis in *Self-Consciousness* (New York: Knopf, 1989), pp. 42-78; the quotation comes from page 48. I quote Wendell Berry from his *Standing by Words* (San Francisco: North Point, 1983), p. 205.

CHAPTER 6: Whose Fidelity? Which Intimacy?

The grim statistics on divorce and the anecdotal material on the greeting cards, liturgies and the like come from Barbara Dafoe Whitehead and David Blankenhorn, "Man, Woman and Public Policy," *First Things,* August/September 1991, pp. 28-35.

Calculation Never Made a Christian Spouse

For more on different conceptions and practices of rationality, see Alasdair MacIntyre, *Whose Justice? Which Rationality?* (Notre Dame, Ind.: University of Notre Dame Press, 1988).

Here and throughout the chapter, for the contrast between covenantal and contractual marriage I am indebted to H. Richard Niebuhr's discussion of covenant in *Faith on Earth* (New Haven, Conn.: Yale University Press, 1989).

Wendell Berry's statement about breaking vows comes from his *Standing by Words* (San Francisco: North Point, 1983), p. 202.

Fidelity as a Bodily Act

In this section I am indebted to Karl Barth's discussion of fidelity in *Church Dogmatics* 3/2, trans. Harold Knight et al. (Edinburgh: T. & T. Clark, 1960),

p. 307. On the Greek view of sex being comparable merely to eating and drinking, see Charles H. Talbert, *Reading Corinthians* (New York: Crossroad, 1987), pp. 29-30. On the complicated relation between the body, the spirit and sexual activity, see the superb study of 1 Corinthians 6:12-20 in Dan O. Via Jr.'s *Self-Deception and Wholeness in Paul and Matthew* (Minneapolis: Fortress, 1990), pp. 66-75; and comments by Gordon Fee, *The First Epistle to the Corinthians* (Grand Rapids, Mich.: Eerdmans, 1987), pp. 255-56.

It is worth pointing out that a presumption for sex within marriage is not exclusive to conservative or evangelical Christians. True enough, evangelicals are more absolutistic (at least rhetorically) about this matter, but for mainline ethicists who clearly understand genital sex contained within public marriage as the Christian ideal, see Gilbert Meilaender, *The Limits of Love* (University Park, Penn.: Pennsylvania State University Press, 1987), pp. 115-30; J. Philip Wogaman, *Christian Moral Judgment* (Louisville, Ky.: Westminster/John Knox, 1989), pp. 154-58; Philip Turner, *Sex, Money and Power* (Cambridge, Mass.: Cowley, 1985); and Waldo Beach, *Christian Ethics in the Protestant Tradition* (Atlanta: John Knox, 1988), pp. 53-64.

How Cohabitation Makes Sense

Lenore Weitzman is quoted in Alan Wolfe, *Whose Keeper? Social Science and Moral Obligation* (Berkeley: University of California Press, 1989), p. 58.

The blessing ceremony of a homosexual couple was reported in Gayle White, "Episcopalians Stand Pat on Homosexuality," *The Christian Century,* August 7-14, 1991, pp. 740-41.

For Wendell Berry's remarks on the marriage as a practice situated within particular communities and traditions, see *Standing by Words,* p. 200.

Making Love, Making Persons

On how sex can be darkly but easily turned into a means of self-gratification, see Reinhold Niebuhr's classic *The Nature and Destiny of Man* (New York: Charles Scribner's Sons, 1964), 1:228-40. For a brilliant treament of how the legal privatization of sex has promoted it as merely a means of self-gratification, see Gerard V. Bradley, "The Constitution and the Erotic Self," *First Things*, October 1991, pp. 28-34.

For an insightful attack on the deterioration of intimacy into a matter of technique, see Wendell Berry, *Home Economics* (San Francisco: North Point, 1987), p. 122.

Gridlock in Wheelchairs

My friend Richard Ecker has since published his thoughts on emotional handicaps in "Whatever Happened to Grace?" *Perspectives,* March 1992, pp. 12-14.

CHAPTER 7: Welcoming Children and Other Strangers
The Suckling Babe as Moral Model

For statistical corroboration of the claim that our society cares too little for its children, see such articles as Charles M. Madigan, "Hard Times for Children in U.S.," *Chicago Tribune,* January 3, 1992, sec. 1, pp. 1 and 12. Madigan cites a recent study by economists Victor Fuchs and Diane Reklis, showing over the last thirty years alarming rates of increase in the number of teen suicides, births to unwed mothers, children living in poverty, children without health insurance and so forth. As Madigan writes, "In almost every area of measurement, from the impact of family instability to scores on standardized college entrance exams, performance of children declined."

Augustine's quote about the demanding infant comes from *The Confessions,* trans. John K. Ryan (Garden City, N.Y.: Image Books, 1960), p. 49 (1. 7).

I quote Michael Thompson from Katharine Davis Fishman, "Therapy for Children," *The Atlantic,* June 1991, pp. 47-81 (quote from p. 48). David Popenoe's comment is found in his "Family Decline in America," *Rebuilding the Nest,* ed. David Blankenhorn et al. (Milwaukee, Wisc.: Family Service America, 1990), p. 45.

Michael Dorris on children holding us hostage comes from his extraordinary and moving account *The Broken Cord* (New York: Harper Perennial, 1989), p. 198.

Hebrews and Other Border-Crossers
Walter Brueggemann's typically insightful and challenging reading of Hebrews as strangers comes from his *Interpretation and Obedience* (Minneapolis: Fortress, 1991), pp. 292-93.

The statement that hospitality was a "pillar of morality" in ancient Israel comes from John Koenig, *New Testament Hospitality* (Philadelphia: Fortress, 1985), p. 2.

Children as Strangers
Historian Lawrence Stone is quoted from his *The Past and the Present Revisited* (London: Routledge and Kegan Paul, 1987), pp. 321-23. For other basically corroborating arguments, see Sarah Blaffer Hrdy, "The Myth of Mother Love," *The New York Times Book Review,* August 30, 1992, p. 11; and Martha Nussbaum, "Justice for Women!" *The New York Review of Books,* October 8, 1992, pp. 43-48.

Village of the Damned (1960) was directed by Wolf Rilla. Of the other works of imagination mentioned here, Doris Lessing's *The Fifth Child* (New York: Vintage, 1988) is the most profound, vividly conveying the darker fears of parenthood in postmodernity.

Four Ways Our Children Are Strangers
Selma Fraiberg's material comes from her witty and supremely helpful

classic *The Magic Years* (New York: Charles Scribner's Sons, 1959), pp. 62-63.

CHAPTER 8: No Christian Home Is a Haven

For helpful feminist insights on the crumbling wall between public and private, see Sara Ruddick, *Maternal Thinking* (Boston: Beacon, 1989); and Mary Stewart Van Leeuwen, "Should Private Morality Go Public? A Christian Feminist Evaluation," *Christian Scholars Review* 22 (September 1992): 36-56.

Elsewhere in this book I have gratefully relied on the work of Wendell Berry. His writing can also be recommended on the point of healing the split between our so-called private and public lives. For instance, Berry is deeply bothered that "modern urban-industrial society is based on a series of radical disconnections between body and soul, husband and wife, marriage and community, community and earth" (*Recollected Essays, 1955-1980* [San Francisco: North Point, 1984], p. 323). And critic Steven Weiland correctly remarks that for Berry "private and public life, love and work are bound historically and practically by the household." Of course, I would want to emend Berry by saying that for Christians the primary or foundational household (family) is not husband and wife in marriage but brother and sister in baptism. (See Weiland, "Wendell Berry: Culture and Fidelity," *Iowa Review* 10 [Winter 1979]: 99-104, quote from 101. This was drawn to my attention by David C. Wright, "The Spirituality of Place: Wendell Berry's Poetry and the Ground of Being," M.A. thesis, Northeast Missouri State University, Kirksville, 1991, p. 62.)

The Wall Falls

Alan Wolfe discusses our paradoxical situation in his *Whose Keeper? Social Science and Moral Obligation* (Berkeley: University of California Press, 1989), p. 5.

Secularization and Divided Lives

John D. Rockefeller is cited in Richard Hofstadter, *Social Darwinism in American Thought* (New York: George Braziller, 1959), p. 45.

For more on this account of secularization as most importantly the division of the public and private worlds, see David Lyon, *The Steeple's Shadow: On the Myths and Realities of Secularization* (Grand Rapids, Mich.: Eerdmans, 1985); and Lesslie Newbigin, *The Gospel in a Pluralist Society* (Grand Rapids, Mich.: Eerdmans, 1989). In *Theology and Social Theory* (London: Basil Blackwell, 1990), John Milbank observes that many traditional religions (including Christianity) make no separation between (private) "religious" and (public) "empirical" reality. The modern "policing of the sublime," in Milbank's words, "exactly coincides with the actual operations of secular society which excludes religion from its modes of 'discipline and control,' while protecting it as a 'private' value" (p. 106). For a helpful discussion of how various thinkers reject modernism's fragmentation of life into such categories as public and private, searching instead for a postmodern holism, see John McGowan, *Postmodernism and Its Critics* (Ithaca, N.Y.: Cornell University Press, 1991). McGowan's account of "semiautonomy" is especially suggestive, and in many ways compatible with the Reformed Christian conception of life lived in distinctive but related "spheres."

The Not-So-Private Households of Rome

For details on the Roman family I have relied mainly on Paul Veyne, ed., *A History of Private Life,* vol. 1, *From Pagan Rome to Byzantium,* trans. Arthur Goldhammer (Cambridge, Mass.: Belknap, 1989), pp. 9-205. Also helpful were David L. Balch, *Let Wives Be Submissive: The Domestic Code in 1 Peter* (Chico, Calif.: Scholars, 1981); and O. Larry Yarbrough, *Not Like the Gentiles: Marriage Rules in the Letters of Paul* (Atlanta: Scholars, 1985).

The Christian Home Is a Mission Base

New Testament scholar Charles H. Talbert offers some helpful words on how the church carries and evidences Christ before the world. Talbert reminds us that the name "Israel" could stand both for the individual Jacob and for the entire community descended from Jacob. Likewise, Paul uses "Christ" to designate both the individual Jesus and the church, the community descended from Jesus. Israel (the people) and Christ (the church) are corporate or group personalities. So, Talbert writes, Paul means that "individual Christians in their corporeal existence are the various body parts of the corporate personality of Christ through which the life of Christ is expressed" (*Reading Corinthians: A Literary and Theological Commentary on 1 and 2 Corinthians* [New York: Crossroad, 1987], pp. 81-95).

Very near the end of this section, I comment that we often make the market into the church. We make the market into the church when we adopt its conceptuality and language to evangelize and serve the world, most blatantly when we "market the church." At a deeper level, we make the market into the church when we give over the conduct of our work life entirely to the standards of the market. Lesslie Newbigin writes:

The chance workings of the free market become the "Invisible Hand" of Adam Smith which mysteriously converts private selfishness into public good. This particular example of an invisible power ruling over human affairs is particularly relevant to the present, since it is one of the key arguments of the religious Right against the religious Left that one cannot speak of justice or injustice when describing the huge differences between rich and poor in our society. These, on this view, cannot be called unjust because they are not the work of conscious human agency but the result of chance. *Thus in our economic life we are no longer responsible to Christ; we are not responsible at all, for economic life has been handed over to the goddess Fortuna.* It is not difficult to recognize that as one of the principalities and powers of which Paul speaks.

See *The Gospel in a Pluralist Society* (Grand Rapids, Mich.: Eerdmans, 1989), pp. 206-7 (emphasis mine).

Chaste Rebels and Other Witnesses

Alasdair MacIntyre writes about chastity in *After Virtue,* 2nd ed. (Notre Dame, Ind.: University of Notre Dame Press, 1984). The Richard B. Hays quote on Habitat for Humanity comes from his "Scripture-Shaped Community: The Problem of Method in New Testament Ethics," *Interpretation* 44 (January 1990): 42-55. I quote M. Craig Barnes from his *Yearning: Living Between How It Is and How It Ought To Be* (Downers Grove, Ill.: InterVarsity Press, 1992), pp. 176-78.

Intimacy Is Not Enough

On how the kingdom should not be made an instrumental aid to the family or any other good, a classic passage from John Howard Yoder is worth recalling:

> If a man repents it will do something for his moral weakness by giving him the focus for wholesome self-discipline, it will keep him from immorality and get him to work on time. So the Peales and the Robertses who promise that God cares about helping me squeeze through the tight spots of life are not wrong; they have their place. BUT ALL OF THIS IS NOT THE GOSPEL. This is just the bonus, the wrapping paper thrown in when you buy the meat, the "everything" which will be added, without our taking thought for it, if we seek first the kingdom of God and His righteousness.

See *The Original Revolution* (Scottdale, Penn.: Herald Press, 1977), p. 32.

Paul Wadell is quoted from his *Friendship and the Moral Life* (Notre Dame, Ind.: University of Notre Dame Press, 1989), p. 60.

The Mission of Celebration

Richard A. Horsley is quoted from his *Jesus and the Spiral of Violence* (San

Francisco: Harper & Row, 1987), p. 178.

On the quality of resonances and "echoes" of the Old Testament in the New Testament, see the provocative treatment of Richard B. Hays, *Echoes of Scripture in the Letters of Paul* (New Haven, Conn.: Yale University Press, 1989). I take permission to suggest my reading of Luke 7:34 from passages such as the following: "While we will continue to recognize Paul's readings of Scripture as abidingly valid figurations, we will also create new figurations out of the texts that Paul read, and we will do so in part by weaving Paul's own writings into the intertextual web, perhaps discerning correspondences that did not occur to Paul himself" (p. 187). Those concerned about hermeneutical checks on such a reading strategy should consult pages 184-91 of Hays's excellent book.

For deeper appreciation of what John Schneider calls the "celebrative Christ," I am indebted to his thoughts in his forthcoming (and not yet titled) book on Christianity and money (Downers Grove, Ill.: InterVarsity Press). Finally, for the understanding that celebration is a part of Christian mission—and not simply a refreshing break to empower us for Christian mission in the real and public world—I have gained from Stanley Hauerwas's wonderful essay "Taking Time for Peace: The Ethical Significance of the Trivial," in his *Christian Existence Today* (Durham, N.C.: Labyrinth, 1988), pp. 253-66.

Burnout: From the Rocket to the Cross

I owe the suggestion that burnout might be reinterpreted to Stanley Hauerwas and William Willimon, "The Limits of Care: Burnout as an Ecclesial Issue," *Word and World,* Summer 1990, pp. 247-53.